Praise for Charles Williams

'Amusingly instructive about the delaying tactics snobbish MCC panjandrums such as Gubby Allen used to prevent the inevitable' *Independent*, Book of the Week

'Fascinating' *Sunday Times*

'Magnificent' *The Cricketer*

'Williams [is] a tailor-made author for a life of Bradman . . . Penetratingly and attractively told'

Roy Jenkins, *Spectator*

'It would be stupid to say I enjoyed or agreed with every word, every sentence and every nuance, but I honestly believe it is a splendid production' Sir Donald Bradman

Charles Williams (Lord Williams of Elvel) is a former Deputy Leader of the Opposition in the House of Lords. He is the acclaimed biographer of De Gaulle, Adenauer, Pétain, Don Bradman and Harold Macmillan.

By Charles Williams

The Last Great Frenchman
Bradman
Adenauer
Pétain
Harold Macmillan
Gentlemen & Players

GENTLEMEN & PLAYERS

The death of amateurism in cricket

CHARLES WILLIAMS

PHOENIX

A PHOENIX PAPERBACK

First published in Great Britain in 2012
by Weidenfeld & Nicolson
This paperback edition published in 2013
by Phoenix,
an imprint of Orion Books Ltd,
Orion House, 5 Upper St Martin's Lane,
London WC2H 9EA

An Hachette UK company

1 3 5 7 9 10 8 6 4 2

A CIP catalogue record for this book
is available from the British Library.

ISBN 978-0-7538-2927-1

Typeset by Input Data Services Ltd, Bridgwater, Somerset

Printed and bound by CPI Group (UK) Ltd, Croydon, CR0 4YY

The Orion Publishing Group's policy is to use papers that
are natural, renewable and recyclable products and
made from wood grown in sustainable forests. The logging
and manufacturing processes are expected to conform to
the environmental regulations of the country of origin.

www.orionbooks.co.uk

For all cricket lovers

Contents

List of Illustrations

Preface

This book is, at least in part, autobiographical. During the middle of the last century I was privileged to play for almost ten years at near to the highest level of English cricket. It is true, I freely confess, that the highest level was beyond my capabilities. This is not false modesty. In cricketing terms there was much to be modest about. For instance, my only appearance for the Gentlemen against the Players, at the Scarborough Festival of 1956, was by any standards undistinguished: 'C. C. P. Williams c Evans b Tyson...0', the scorecard of the first innings reads, and, in the second innings, things were no better: 'b Shepherd 1'. Nevertheless, to play, even in a minor role, with or against the Prince Hamlets of the day, Len Hutton, Alec Bedser, Peter May, Doug Insole, Denis Compton, Bill Edrich, Jim Laker, Colin Cowdrey, Trevor Bailey, Frank Tyson, Brian Statham, Richie Benaud, Ray Lindwall, Keith Miller and all the others in cricket's hall of fame is something that in my boyhood I would have said to be beyond any of my most exciting dreams. My Oxford boyhood, as it happens, and my later memories provide a convenient frame for the picture as I paint it in the book.

What is not autobiographical is my description of the long process which, during my first-class cricketing career, led to a fundamental change in the structure of the game. In fact, I am one of a now sadly diminishing band who played as true amateurs, only for the love of the game. In short, not to put too fine a point on it, I am something of a dinosaur.

There is no doubt that the Second World War brought great changes in society as a whole and, consequentially, in sports. The whole structure of officers and other ranks – gentlemen and professionals – built so carefully by our Victorian ancestors and nurtured during the First World War and its aftermath, and even surviving to the end of the Second World War, had started to weaken. Cricket, like other sports, in the end came to the conclusion that the structure itself could not hold up. By 1962, the Marylebone Cricket Club faced what seemed by then to be the inevitable. Other sports had already moved or were quick to follow suit. The distinction between 'amateur' and 'professional' had to go. As one of the last of the 'amateurs' – the dinosaurs – I have to bow my head in acknowledgement of justifiable extinction.

Yet there is a link between autobiography and analysis. Although we players were only dimly aware at the time that the issues of amateurism and professionalism were being debated, we knew the cast of characters involved – not least because many of them were players alongside us or against us. Doug Insole, my captain at Essex, to take one example, was a consistently prominent player both on the field and in the debating rooms. That an author has known personally, as I did, those involved in both activities allows characters who appear unidimensional in the printed record to become human beings of flesh and blood in the telling. Of course, the historically minded autobiographer, with his, or her, fragile memory, is bound to seek support from outside sources. With much help from others, this is what I have tried to do. It is therefore an ensuing mix of personal recollection and verifiable fact which I try to present and which, I hope, is one that will commend itself to the reader.

A passing thought, however, occurs by way of an *obiter dictum*. With the death of amateurism in first-class cricket – and, almost simultaneously, in other sports – it may well be that we, as a society, have lost something valuable. In its final form, as I try to point out, amateurism in the highest levels of cricket became so ludicrous in its presentation and corrupt in its practice that it had to go. Nevertheless there were features of amateurism – the Corinthian spirit, if you like, as it used to be called, where the only object was to play a game with honour and verve – that we may regret having thrown overboard. Perhaps – who knows? – the dinosaurs may have had a point.

I

THE WALK TO THE PARKS

Et in Arcadia ego

It was a long walk for an eight-year-old boy. My route was simple and unchanging from day to day. I used to leave my home in Christ Church early to walk to school – in the 1940s, in the Oxford wartime, I was not yet trusted with a bicycle. I went along the eastern side of Tom Quad, with my satchel on my back, through Canterbury Gate, past Oriel College, across the broad and sometimes dangerous expanse of the High Street, then into the Turl, along the length of Parks Road, on through the tree-lined streets of North Oxford, past the smug gardens of Norham Road and so to my destination. At the end of the school day I walked back along the same route, back to Christ Church and the friendly greetings of the porter at Canterbury Gate, and finally to my home in the Priory House.

It was always, even when the weather was bad, a pleasant enough walk, although it was lonely and, in the imagination of a young boy, fraught with danger. But apart from largely imagined dangers, such as ghosts (or unruly evacuees), it turned out to be safer than almost anywhere

1

else in the south of England. Exciting as it was to watch in the high summer of 1940 the vapour trails of the fighter aircraft as they fought out their desperate battle it was comforting to know that the bombs were falling elsewhere. Oxford seemed to be under some sort of divine protection (not least, as became apparent, because Adolf Hitler had marked the city down as his capital after the impending German occupation). People in the streets, too, were always friendly to the young schoolboy as he went on his way. Yet my route, as it was day after day, is etched in my memory for a different reason. On a particular day, 11 May 1943, I was called out of class to be told by one of the masters, with the greatest sympathy and gentleness, that my father had died. I was therefore, he said, given leave to go home. Did I want somebody to take me? Give me a lift? I replied that I would rather walk. I remember that the sun was shining as I went back along the familiar route. But it was without any doubt the longest and saddest walk of my life.

Eleven years later all had changed. The route was the same and the sun seemed to shine as before. But by then I was a fully fledged undergraduate at Christ Church and in charge of my own bicycle. The bicycle route came to its end, not at my old school, but at the Oxford University cricket ground in the University Parks. I had been selected to play cricket for Oxford, an honour previously beyond imagining. Those who know the ground and the Parks themselves will be familiar with the place. The ground was, and still is, a place of beauty, simple in its surroundings, without a suggestion of an obtrusive stand for those who wish to watch the cricket. As now, people could come and go as they please, and, if so minded, stay and watch.

After the Second World War there had been some much-needed restoration. The pavilion had just about survived the neglect of the war period and a new grounds-man had rescued the outfield from the weeds which had overgrown it. By the time I appeared on the scene the pavilion and ground was reasonably well – if not quite wholly – restored. But at least it was ready for what was for me a great event. On 12 May 1954, the day after the elev-enth anniversary of my father's death, the record shows that the great M. C. Cowdrey and C. C. P. Williams put on 173 runs for Oxford University against Lancashire for the third wicket. The sun had shone as never before. To cap it all, E. W. Swanton wrote in the following day's *Daily Telegraph* that there were times when he could not spot the difference between Williams and Cowdrey.

Quite apart from the cricket, there was a more mun-dane reason why Swanton was unable to tell the differ-ence between the two of us. Both, as it happened, were wearing Harlequin caps. This was no accident. Although the cap itself now seems to have gone out of fashion, in its day it was widely worn by Oxford Blues and near Blues. It was much admired, like a peacock, for its gothic triangles of Oxford blue, magenta and gold (or maroon and buff or crimson and beige – the descriptions vary) reaching their point at a button on the top of the head. As such, it was in itself, as it was intended to be, a statement of crick-eting flamboyance (in their first match the Harlequins not only wore trousers of Oxford blue but also shirts of maroon/magenta and buff/gold – the first known example of cricket in pyjamas).

Not that the award of a Harlequin was achieved easily. The first and paramount condition was that the candidate had to have played at least one first-class match. Quite who decided on the award was never entirely clear to us. The club had a committee with apparently plenipotentiary powers, but the successful candidates then somehow just seemed to emerge. Nevertheless, it was an award which carried with it not just the wearing of a cap but a measure of distinction. The club, such as it was, had after all been founded in 1852, a year after the Cambridge equivalent (Quidnuncs) and around the same time as the better known I Zingari. Its purpose had been, and to some extent still was, to encourage at Oxford the spirit of amateur cricket which had taken hold in the public schools during the mid-Victorian period. Since it was considered unseemly, pending further selection for the current year, to wear a Blue cap won the previous summer, and since wearing an 'Authentics' cap (for the Oxford 2nd XI) was to downgrade, the Harlequin was the best available option. Furthermore, it demonstrated, for those who cared, the amateur and public school dominance of the cricket world at large. Finally, it had been worn almost *in perpetuo* by Douglas Jardine specifically, it seemed, to irritate the Australians. That in itself gave it unlimited cachet.

It was, of course, a mistake to wear a Harlequin cap when playing against certain counties. Yorkshire was a case in point, particularly when F. S. Trueman was playing. The unwise wearer of the cap, as he walked in to bat in the Parks in early May 1954, was greeted with not just the customary Yorkshire unpleasantness but a verbal onslaught from Trueman about the 'jazz 'at' and how

4

he would soon remove it. There followed three bouncers – all three accurately aimed at the Harlequin cap. In the days before helmets it required a nimble neck from the undergraduate to avoid having his head knocked off. But Trueman was the winner. It was C. C. P. Williams b Trueman ... 0, followed by M. C. Cowdrey (also in a Harlequin cap) c sub b Trueman ... 0. (One of them, at least, redeemed himself in the second innings: C. C. P. Williams c Watson b Illingworth ... 53.)

It was not just a matter of flamboyance in cricket headgear. Oxford in the early 1950s seemed generally to be trying to recapture the perceived insouciance of the pre-war years. In fact, it had been a similar story after the First World War. Then, as the first grim-faced veterans returned home and the stories of the trenches, gas, shell shock and the sheer scale of human sacrifice started to circulate more freely, their presence – and the reluctance of many of them to talk about the wartime horror – cast a gloom over those who had been left behind. Gradually, however, the generation of young men who had not fought in the war, and their female companions (or in some cases their male companions), started to assert the hedonism which they thought had died in 1914. Dances became more hectic, music more fragmented, speculation more frenetic and louche behaviour more tolerated. Underlying it all, however, it was possible to note, and has been noted, that the horror for them had only been avoided by a matter of a few years and that there was a sense of guilt that they had not been there to fight. *Brideshead Revisited*, for all its charm, is at bottom a profoundly disturbing portrait of the period.

After the end of the Second World War the phenom-
enon repeated itself, albeit in a different form. There was
not so much horror to be told, but many of those who
came back from the war just wanted nothing further to do
with it, and others, particularly officers, wanted to complete their higher education which had been interrupted
by conscription with as little fuss as possible. The result
was that in the late 1940s Oxford became home to many
of those relatively old soldiers. Some of them, of course,
were sportsmen as well as scholars – the Oxford cricket
team in 1947, for instance, was largely composed of ex-
servicemen in their twenties. Nor was there much jollity.
The old soldiers were serious. Times were generally hard
and they were in no mood to do much more than study
hard and, if necessary, play hard.

That tide took some time to ebb. But by the early 1950s
a younger generation, which had missed war service, was
in its flood. As in the 1920s the ambition was different.
Although National Service in most cases served to tone
down the worst of post-adolescent high spirits, there was
much more of a sense of fun and, indeed, youthful irre-
sponsibility. The undergraduate parties became more
alcoholic and libidinous (although the bizarre male to
female numerical relationship and the absence of a con-
traceptive pill, not yet invented, inhibited what would
now be regarded as normal undergraduate sexual activity – beware, we were told, the unwanted pregnancy),
clubs were reconstituted, Commemoration Balls became
more drunken, the Bullingdon, the dining club reserved
for those who regarded themselves as the social elite,
rampaged again and, so it seemed, work was taken less

seriously. The tutor for Honour Moderations (Mods) at Christ Church, for instance, who had spent a large part of the war in a Japanese prisoner-of-war camp, regarded sharing a glass of sherry with his pupil in what was meant to be a tutorial as more important than the study of Homer.

What was clearly evident, however, and common to the 1920s and the 1950s, was a sense of elitism. After all, in both periods only some 5 per cent of those leaving secondary school went on to higher education – and Oxford and Cambridge were still the pinnacles of ambition. It is no surprise that those who reached the summits thought – and to a large extent were encouraged to think – that they were the elite who would provide the future ruling class. Of course it was not just the influence of higher education. The public schools (or 'fee-paying schools' as they might more properly be known) provided the bulk of entrants to Oxford and Cambridge. The elitism there was the same. Finally, although the war had served to break down some of the class barriers between officers and men, those of us who did our National Service in the 1950s found those barriers fully re-established. In short, the officers were 'gentlemen' and the other ranks 'players'. We young men were left in no doubt that we were the young 'gentlemen'. We had yet to discover who the players were.

Each spring the Oxford University Cricket Club (OUCC) formally invited a number of prospective candidates for future selection to play for the University. They were to present themselves in the Parks for nets. The candidates were those who had shone the previous year or, if they were freshmen, who had shone in the public schools season the year before or, alternatively, who had come with a reputation from Australia, New Zealand or South Africa. The data on which the invitations were based could easily be found on the *Wisden* record. The seasons of all the major – and some not so major – public schools were published, as were full records of the matches 'Southern vs Northern Schools' and the subsequent 'Public Schools vs Combined Services', both of which were, with some fanfare, played at Lord's.

The selection of candidates for the early season nets thus followed a predictable path. In fact, the public school boys and overseas students were almost always better than those coming up through the English state system. The roll call of British schools attended by those who were eventually selected for the Oxford vs Cambridge match in early July 1954 makes the point: Charterhouse, Wellington, Westminster, Rossall, Tonbridge, Edinburgh Academy, Stamford, Dulwich, Christ's Hospital, Alleyn's, Brighton, Marlborough. But this was hardly surprising. Apart from Westminster, whose main playing field at Vincent Square had been an emplacement for barrage balloons – although the cricket square had been avoided thanks to the initiative of the commanding officer (my uncle) – these schools had the best facilities, reasonably good coaching and an ethos which gave sport primacy over more intellectual pursuits. The public school boys thus enjoyed sporting advantages which the state schools simply could not match.

The selection made, the successful candidates then presented themselves. It was an unusually cold May morning which greeted the selected candidates of 1952 – such as myself – as we nervously turned up in the Parks with whatever decent equipment we could muster. We were met by two professional coaches: Jack Walsh, an Australian who played for Leicestershire, and 'Lofty' Herman, retired from Hampshire. It turned out that their main function was to assess the ability of each candidate and advise on which of them should be selected to play for the University and at which level.

The relationship between candidate and coach was not altogether easy. Those who had finished their National Service compared it to the relationship between officer cadets and regimental sergeant majors at an Officer Cadet Training Unit. (The coaches had the unnerving habit of calling the undergraduates 'sir'.) Yet 'Jack' and 'Lofty', as we came to know them, made every possible effort to do what they were paid to do by a mixture of charm and light discipline. In the evenings there was the possibility of a beer or two and to hear stories, jokes and myths of the grown-up cricketing world of which we were on the fringe and which we hoped to enter. We enjoyed the banter – but knew that we were being judged.

Sooner or later, the time came to face the grown-ups in person on the battlefield. It was certainly daunting. Almost all counties fielded their strongest, or near strongest, sides against both Oxford and Cambridge at the time. Although it was seen as an opportunity to try out younger professionals, there was little appetite for what would be a humiliating defeat. The result was that the young amateurs were taught some salutary lessons. Instead of playing off spin on a turning wicket by pushing the bat forward in front of the pad (as taught at school), for instance, we learnt to play behind the pad to avoid the catch to short leg. Instead of expecting wickets to fall like ninepins we learnt to field to opposing stands of 100 or 150 without losing patience – or dropping catches at crucial moments. Instead of looking to the next interval we learnt to field through a whole day without a murmur. In short, in cricketing terms we were growing up.

We were growing up, too, in other ways. As the day of examinations approached there was a matter of correcting the idleness of earlier months and settling down to academic work. Some, of course, did not bother. Colin Cowdrey, for instance, never felt it necessary to take more than a cursory examination, reckoning that his career prospects were best served by playing cricket rather than sitting what for him would be a forlorn test for a degree – and that he was too valuable to Oxford to be sent down. (He was right on both counts.) Others did the minimum necessary to maintain their presence. Those of us who were more worried about getting a good degree had to work out a system during the cricket season. After fielding all day or batting for long hours it was not sensible to sit down to write an essay or construe a piece of Greek prose. The only option was to get up early in the morning – say, at six o'clock – and put in four hours' work before turning the mind's attention to cricket.

The summer term ended and the season for examinations past, the Oxford side went on tour to prepare for the encounter with Cambridge at Lord's, normally in early July. Touring brought its own problems. Unlike county sides which moved about constantly and were correspondingly well organised, university sides had to make shift – with the consequent frequent chaos in the practical arrangements. Besides, the tour came at the end of term at precisely the time when the summer Balls took place, which was annoying, to say the least, for those who wished to join in the most lively expressions of undergraduate *joie de vivre* – and an opportunity to survey the large group of London girls who descended on Oxford for the occasion. In fact, such was the enthusiasm that on occasions the touring cricketers would stay in Oxford overnight and turn up to play wherever it might be the following morning. (I remember one such time in 1952, when I stayed for the Christ Church Commem Ball, drove with friends in the early morning to Worthing for the game against Sussex – and made 74 in the first innings the same morning.)

Such frivolity came to an end as attention became more and more focused on the University match. Not that it was a particularly disciplined focus. There were no batting coaches, fielding coaches, bowling coaches, fitness coaches or sports psychologists. There was only one harassed don accompanying the team. Once in London we stayed where we wished, mostly with friends or family. As long as we turned up at Lord's at the right time on the right day (not always guaranteed) that was good enough.

Once at Lord's, however, the atmosphere changed. The match, against the old enemy, was always deeply competitive – and sometimes bad-tempered. Nerves, too, took over. Added to that, the flooring in the Lord's pavilion had (and still has, but it was much more marked sixty years ago) an unpleasant smell which did nothing for the batsman's stomach as he descended the stairs from the dressing room and crossed the Long Room on his way to the wicket in front of some 10,000 spectators. In truth, it was never a match to be enjoyed. It just had to be played as part of the price of glory in winning a Blue and appearing to the rest of the undergraduate world as a hero.

No sooner was the match over than those of us who were eligible to play for our counties waited for invitations to do so. But when the summons came it turned out to be a particularly delicate matter. We would play as amateurs but we soon learnt that we would be dislodging professionals and thus, putting it brutally, making it more difficult for them to earn their living. Indeed, it was even worse than that. Amateurs, unless they were bound by their positions as captain, could come and go as they wished. If an amateur wished to go on holiday he could tell his county Secretary that he would not be available between one date and another. After that, he would be available to return to the side. The flood of public schoolmasters and University Blues, at the end of their respective terms, made the job of selectors – each county had its own committee, normally presided over by the appointed captain but with the senior professional at hand – not just a matter of relative ability but of maintaining a calendar detailing when the amateurs decided that they were available and when they decided that they were not. It was the bad fortune of the professionals who were marginal players in the county side that they were from time to time bounced out simply because an amateur declared himself available for a particular game.

That said, at least at Essex, where I played in the University vacation, the professionals seemed to take all this as no more and no less than another fact of life, and went out of their way to welcome the raw recruit from Oxford. There was no question of separate dressing rooms (as at the Oval). We huddled down in whatever shed was available. The simple reason was that in those days Essex played on local club grounds – there was no 'county ground' as such. There were weeks in Westcliff, Ilford, Brentwood, Romford, Chelmsford, Colchester, Clacton and Southend. Although the wickets were always different – and needed different batting and bowling techniques to deal with them – one thing was constant: we all changed in the same hut. There was no 'them and us'. Not only did this serve to promote team spirit but it made the younger amateurs sharper in their determination to show their professional colleagues that they were worthy members of the team.

To some extent ranks broke when we went to play away games. The fixture schedules were demanding to the point of absurdity. In June 1954, for instance, Essex, always finishing at six o'clock and starting the next morning generally at half past eleven, went from Brentwood on the 11th to Rushden in Northamptonshire, then immediately after playing for three days there (and a charity match, as usual, on the Sunday) to Liverpool on the 15th, then back to Romford on the 18th, to Gloucester on the 25th, Ebbw Vale on the 29th, back to Blackheath on 2 July and Chelmsford on the 6th. In August the same year we went from Clacton on the 10th to Scarborough, on the 13th to Weston-super-Mare and then immediately back to play at Southend. Almost all these journeys involved driving over 100 miles well into the night on pre-motorway roads. Nor were we the exception. Other counties could tell a similar story. Glamorgan, for instance, in July of the same year, went from Llanelli to Nottingham, back to Ebbw Vale, on to Peterborough, down to the Oval and then back to Swansea. It is little wonder that players, after arriving in the middle of the night or the early morning and having to turn out for a day's cricket, at times actively prayed for rain.

The richer counties, or those supported by local industry, such as Warwickshire, Leicestershire, Northamptonshire or Yorkshire, were able to afford coaches to take their sides hither and thither. Those that were less well off – or downright poor, like Essex – relied on volunteers among the team to drive their own cars. In the days when there were no motorways this was always a dangerous enterprise. The bags were entrusted to the scorer who usually set off later than the rest of the team (and frequently lost his way). The others piled into whatever car they were offered. In the Essex side the amateurs tended to gravitate together towards the car of the (amateur) captain, Doug Insole. In terms of safety on the road, many of us realised too late that this might be a bad mistake, since Doug was, to say the least, a most aggressive driver and caused us many moments of the sheerest terror. We were reassured, however, at least in part, by the fact that our driver, on our stops for supper at some pub or other, only drank ginger beer.

Amateurs and professionals generally stayed at the same hotel. In truth, in those days there was not very much choice. The difficulty was that all the expenses of the amateurs were met by the club while the professionals had to pay for themselves. Inevitably this led from time to time to separation between the two groups in evening excursions (although we were all of us welcome guests at

Butlins in Clacton). Once on the field, however, even in the charity matches on Sundays, the distinction was set aside.

All the county sides had their 'characters'. Among the favourites at Essex was our opening bat, T. C. ('Dickie') Dodds. He was a kindly and gentle soul, and a devotee of the Moral Re-Armament movement founded before the war by the American priest Frank Buchman, so much so that, during the winters, he used to spend time at its head-quarters at Caux in Switzerland. His devotion, however, led him to strange places, not least to the practice of kneeling in prayer in the dressing room before going out to bat. The rest of us tremulously agreed that he was receiving a message from the Almighty about what sort of innings he should play. Since he was an aggressive batsman – and a fine striker of the ball – we all waited to see, with much trepidation, what that message would be and how Dickie would interpret it. It was always tense – and sometimes disastrous. On one occasion Dickie had clearly been told that the first two balls of the innings, from our opponents' fastest bowler, would be half-volleys. They were indeed – and were duly struck back over the bowler's head for four. Unfortunately the Almighty seemed to have told Dickie that the next ball would be a bouncer. Dickie shaped to hook only to find that it was a yorker – and his stumps were scattered all over the place, as one member put it, 'like autumn leaves in Vallombrosa'. The bowler was fired up to boiling point and the batsman next in – myself, as it happened – trudged to the wicket with what can only be described as sickening apprehension.

Trevor Bailey, too, was certainly a 'character'. He was

also the outstanding English all-rounder at the time, a fine defensive batsman, an accurate and aggressive fast-medium bowler and an agile fielder. But he could throw spectacular tantrums. Known as the 'Boil' (on a scorecard early in his career he had been fatally misspelt as 'T. E. Boiley'), he was not one to tolerate catches dropped at leg slip to his bowling. His invective was not very imaginative but in its straightforward way conveyed adequately what he thought. Then we had 'Tonker' Taylor, the boy from West Ham who took over from the Yorkshireman Paul Gibb as our wicketkeeper, nicknamed so because of his habit of trying to hit every ball out of sight; 'Strangler' Ralph, possibly so called because he resembled a murderer much in the news at the time; 'Casey' Preston, our senior professional and a fine bowler of fast-medium inswing; and 'Smudger' Smith, another senior who insisted on wearing his cap at a jaunty angle and was never short of words calculated to irritate the opposition. Even I had my soubriquet: because of my rather lugubrious disposition I was known as 'Cheerful Charlie'.

All in all, Essex in the 1950s was a good-tempered and a happy side. Others – notably Yorkshire, Surrey and Glamorgan – could have their rows and sulks, as they did, but we managed to avoid them. Yet for the inquisitive mind there was always the matter of why players were divided into amateurs and professionals, why amateurs could dislodge professionals at will, why some spoke with one voice and some with another, why captains were almost (though not quite) always amateurs, or, not least, why the game was run by the aged and self-important middle class who were our club members and who made up the membership of the Marylebone Cricket Club (MCC). There was much to consider and, as my salad days came to their inevitable end, I did indeed start seriously to reflect on the game I was playing. As it happened, my reflections led me from time to time into strange territory.

2

THE GENTLEMEN

*Gentleman: a man of chivalrous instincts
and fine feelings (OED)*

In the now unimaginable world before plasma television screens and digital photography, in other words in the 1930s, we children used to collect cigarette cards. These were retrieved, by hook or by dastardly crook, from the packets of cigarettes bought by our adults before they were – after the contents had been duly smoked – negligently thrown away. Our motive was simple. The cards were colour pictures, admittedly idealised, of the faces of (among others) our favourite sportsmen. However imperfect they were, it was the only practicable way for us to know what our heroes looked like. If a cricket-loving boy wanted to know about the appearance of, for example, W. R. Hammond or K. S. Ranjitsinhji, apart from the almost impossible feat of confronting the great man when he was playing, the cigarette card was the only option.

But it was a chancy business. The adults (who covered a wide range of parents, porters, chefs and other friendly staff at Christ Church) might not be able to produce the one important card which was missing and vital to the collection. In that case there was another method of acquisition open – to go into what was an active secondary market with other children with similar problems and swap our superfluous cards for the one which we coveted and which they were prepared to relinquish. The negotiations, however, could from time to time be difficult – and even bad-tempered. One 'Bradman', for instance, could normally command at least three 'Rhodes' (but on a good day four). It depended on the time and day (and, often, on the relative physical strengths of the negotiators). All in all, it was, as the cigarette manufacturers intended, a thriving business which probably led to children encouraging their adults to buy, and to smoke, more cigarettes. In fact, collections could over the years run into more than one, and sometimes two, hundred cards. Naturally, as the size of collections grew, for ease of access they were frequently classified into different categories by their enthusiastic proprietors. For cricketing boys one such classification was into 'gentlemen' and 'players', in other words 'amateurs' and 'professionals'.

This brought its own problems. Although in the 1930s it was possible to identify amateurs by reading the cricket scores in the newspapers and noting those players whose initials preceded their surnames ('gentlemen') as opposed to those whose initials followed their surname ('players'), there were mistakes. Furthermore, as we grew up we learnt that not all amateurs were necessarily 'gentlemen' as we had been taught to understand the word. There had been, and still were, villains and cheats among them (the heroic Grace brothers, W. G. and E. M., for instance, seemed on investigation to figure in both categories). What bothered us most was by what mechanism 'amateurs' should have been able to assume the mantle of 'gentlemen' and why – confusingly – 'gentlemen' were regarded with almost reverential respect.

The second question was easier to answer than the first. The answer – like the answers to so many other questions about England – had its roots deep in the English class system. There were, we learnt, many attributes which marked a person as being a 'gentleman' or a 'lady' – dress, deportment, manners, mode of speech – but there was no doubt that speech was the most immediately arresting. In the later years of the reign of Queen Victoria and into the twentieth century almost all 'gentlemen' and 'ladies' spoke English with what can only be described as a marked nasal drawl. Words such as 'off', 'gone', 'often' and so on were pronounced 'orff', 'gorn', 'orfen'. This way of speaking was instantly recognisable as that of an acceptable member of the class – and hence of the amateur spirit which, it was generally agreed, the class represented. It was, after all, the way the Royal Family spoke (give or take the odd German accent) and could not therefore be challenged. Those who spoke with other accents, such as regional brogues, had to prove themselves to be 'gentlemen' or 'ladies' by other means.

Over the centuries, of course, the English upper class had become accustomed to their own opinion that they were born to be natural leaders. They had, after all, been told so almost endlessly at their public schools. Cricket was merely one case in point. The principle went well beyond that. It permeated government and, with perhaps even more alarming results, the armed forces. The

Crimean War serves as only one unhappy illustration. The gentlemen were officers, whatever their competence, and the rest were other ranks. Later on, both in the Boer War and in the First World War, gentlemen again almost automatically became officers while others took their due place, equally automatically, as other ranks. With the Second World War came – to some extent and only on the surface – change. The divide between 'gentlemen' and 'players' became much less marked, particularly, perhaps because it was the junior service, in the Royal Air Force. Professional cricketers such as L. E. G. Ames and D. V. P. Wright joined the amateurs S. C. Griffith, R. T. Simpson, T. E. Bailey, W. R. Hammond and R. W. V. Robins with commissions (but left behind in the other ranks were Sergeants T. G. Evans and C. Washbrook, Flight Sergeant A. V. Bedser and Lance Corporal D. C. S. Compton).

During the war cricket was still played, and indeed was encouraged by the authorities since the proceeds went to services' charity and the game was also said, rather nebulously, to contribute to national morale. In practice, all the wartime performers, paid as servicemen not as cricketers, played as amateurs. None were paid more than minimal additional expenses for their appearances and only then when their appearance could guarantee a boost in the resulting income for the designated charity. In this spirit Derbyshire, Lancashire and Nottinghamshire organised their own competitions, MCC teams continued to provide games of near first-class standard and the services produced sides made up of those on leave. Also in this spirit, an England team played 'The Dominions' at

Lord's in August 1943 and played against 'Australia', also at Lord's in early August 1944 (Flight Lieutenant W. R. Hammond made 105 for England and Pilot Officer K. R. Miller made 85 for Australia). All this was enough for the editor of the 1943 *Wisden*, the cricketer's ongoing bible, to argue for the ending of the amateur/professional divide for good.

None of that, however, was of much account after the war had ended. The old divide was reasserted. In anticipation – and symbolically – the historic match of Gentlemen vs Players was revived at Lord's as a two-day fixture in late August 1944. As it happened, the result was far from encouraging – the Players (professionals) won by an innings and 140 runs. Undeterred, the MCC insisted on keeping the fixture in the Lord's calendar for 1947 and thereafter, and it was adopted at the Scarborough Festival as a feature for the end of the season.

However retrograde on the face of it, there turned out, almost fortuitously, to be a good reason for the decision. It may initially have been a question of reviving – in the pursuit of the return to normalcy after the war – one of the oldest fixtures in the first-class game. Yet the Gentlemen could field batsmen, such as W. R. Hammond and W. J. Edrich, who could measure up to the professional bowling without discomfort. Moreover, fortune worked in favour of the fixture. Later on, in the late 1940s and early 1950s, Hammond and Edrich (neither of whom were entirely genuine amateurs, having turned from professional status in the hope of being appointed captain of England, although only Hammond achieved his objective) were joined by a group of genuine amateurs –

G. H. G. Doggart, J. G. Dewes, R. T. Simpson, D. J. Insole, M. C. Cowdrey, P. B. H. May and D. S. Sheppard. All of them were batsmen of the highest calibre able to take on the professional bowlers with ease. Furthermore, in T. E. Bailey the amateurs had a bowler who on his day could dismiss even the best of the professional batsmen. It is hardly surprising that in the 1950s the two Gentlemen vs Players matches came to be regarded as trials for selection to the England Test side and the MCC touring sides.

For a boy at the end of the war all this was in the future. We were growing up fast, myself in a household ecclesiastical in nature but which would if asked have probably described itself as on the upper edge of the middle class or even the lower edge of the upper class. The educational ladder was fixed more or less from birth – as was our mode of speech. Preparatory school, public school (scholarship obligatory because of lack of money), Oxford or Cambridge (scholarship again obligatory for the same reason) – all were simply regarded as introductory to the life we were destined to lead in the service of our class (whatever that was) and our country – even, perhaps, in that order. We were taught to speak what was by then the King's English and to be officers and gentlemen. (It took many years for us to adjust our English pronunciation to more convenient use.) It was easy enough to adjust to being officers – our uncles and cousins who fought in the war saw to that – but we were still uncertain about 'gentlemen' and why, in particular, amateur cricketers were so qualified.

For those of us who were enthusiastic – almost desperately so – about cricket there was an additional problem.

Sorting the cigarette cards between 'gentlemen' and 'players' revealed the dreaded secret that some of the amateurs could not possibly be regarded as 'gentlemen' as we knew it. It was not just a matter of the Grace brothers. The Australian international players were amateurs – even Bradman had to live off expenses until he could get back to Australia and cash in through journalism and sponsorship from General Motors – but they did not sound or act like 'gentlemen'. It was, as any boy would have said at the time, most perplexing.

Of course, we all had our heroes and as we grew into the higher reaches of public school cricket and then into first-class game we were happy to learn from them – and do our best to imitate them. Of all the amateur batsmen of the post-war generation the two most enthralling for us to watch – and the most difficult to field against – were Peter May and Colin Cowdrey. Of those two, those of us who played against him and with him would perhaps award the crown to Peter May. He was, as anyone who saw him play will freely agree, a gem of a batsman. Of course, he had all the advantages: he was too young to have fought in the war (although he dutifully did his post-war National Service); he was brought up in a comfortable middle-class family in a tradition of sporting achievement; educated at Charterhouse School – with its perfect batting wickets – and then at Cambridge – on the (near) perfect wicket of Fenner's.

May was in the classic tradition of English batsmanship. As far as possible he played off the front foot – but he was quick to go back when faced with a fast bouncer or a shorter ball from a slow bowler. His left elbow always stayed high when he was on the front foot, particularly so when he went into his cover drive, opening the face of the bat to take the ball past the cover fielders. There was no need to play the hook shot – which, anyway, if the ball lifted, was dangerous in the days before the introduction of protective helmets – and the cut, whether square or late, was not a shot to be played until the eye was fully in. Above all, May excelled in the building of an innings. Statistically, his performance was certainly impressive. His average in Tests was 46.77 and in all first-class matches 51.00; but it is not just in the figures that he should be remembered. All of us who saw him – and who fielded against him – would agree that he was the most elegant batsman of his generation.

He was also a modest and agreeable companion. His brother, John, was also a fine athlete, but more robust in his dealings with the sometimes hostile world. Peter was withdrawn   polite, well-mannered, but strangely inarticulate for a former Charterhouse schoolboy. Moreover, his health was never good. He was plagued with stomach ulcers (and occasionally had to leave the pitch to be sick) and caught colds easily. It somehow sums up his delicate physique to know that he died of a brain tumour at the early age of sixty-four. Sadly – and unfairly – he was never honoured as he should have been. There was a CBE but no knighthood and certainly no peerage.

Colin Cowdrey, by contrast, was showered with honours. Like Peter May, he averaged over forty in Tests at 44.06 but, unlike May, only just over forty, at 42.89 in all first-class matches. Yet he was not just awarded a CBE. There followed a knighthood, then a peerage, and then, in a unique event for a cricketer, a memorial service in Westminster Abbey, with the MCC flag flying over it and within it an address by a former Prime Minister. Those of us who attended, and who had played with him and other great cricketers, could only reflect that perhaps Cowdrey's equals in the English game – Len Hutton, Denis Compton, Peter May or Alec Bedser – might have merited the same.

But they did not have the same connections. Cowdrey was born – in Bangalore in India – into what can only be described as the cricket purple. His father insisted that his initials should be those of the MCC and he was so named (his first name was Michael). Like Peter May he was public school-educated – at Tonbridge, where he was coached by the veteran and great England fast-medium bowler Maurice Tate. At the age of thirteen he played at Lord's in 1946 for Tonbridge against Clifton and then went on to Oxford in 1951 on a Heath Harrison Scholarship to Brasenose College (a scholarship specifically for sportsmen). It was a short jump from there to the MCC team to tour Australia and New Zealand in 1954–5.

Although he won a rackets Blue at Oxford in his first year, Cowdrey's physique was not that of a natural athlete. His feet always caused problems (and required a number of surgical operations) and he was given to lying down to fall asleep in dressing rooms while waiting to go in to bat – hence his nickname 'Kipper'. Moreover, unlike the slim Peter May, he was congenitally overweight. Apart from all else, this made running between the wickets for his batting partners something of a hazard. But his weight did help in what was the stroke for which he is remembered

– recorded, as it happens, in the inscription on his grave-
stone – the cover drive. He would lean into it effortlessly
and his weight and his sense of timing ensured that whoever was fielding at cover point would believe that he had
an easy ball to field until it turned out that the ball had
seemingly accelerated, had passed him and had by that
time hit the boundary rope.

As a person and a personal friend, Cowdrey was not
always easy. With his equals he was courteous but without
being effusive – not at all, as the jargon of the time had it,
a bundle of fun. He could be vague and imprecise about
fulfilling his commitments. With professional cricketers he
was distant and, some would say, arrogant. There was, for
instance, a widely reported confrontation on an Ashes tour
with Ray Illingworth, the Yorkshire professional, whom
Cowdrey apparently commanded to bowl to him in the
nets (not a recommended approach to a Yorkshireman).
Les Ames, the Kent wicketkeeper who played many years
in the same team, is said at one point to have refrained
from writing his cricketing memoirs because he would
have been compelled in honesty to be too rude about
Cowdrey, whom he thought to be the worst form of snob.
Others at Kent thought the same, although they were
too timid to say so. There were whispers, too, about his
two marriages, one to Penny Chiesman, daughter of the
owner of the Kent retailing chain, and the second to the
eldest daughter of the 16th Duke of Norfolk. Apart from
the political networks which opened up to him by virtue
of his two marriages, both in their turn ensured that he
never needed to put in a request for expenses for playing cricket. Finally, Don Bradman, for his part, although

he liked Cowdrey personally, thought caustically that if there was a fence on which it was possible to sit, Cowdrey would be there sitting on it.

Nevertheless, whatever their varying personal characteristics, both May and Cowdrey were, in the very best tradition of the English public school, impeccably well-mannered. They may not have been quite 'gentlemen' in the late Victorian sense but they certainly passed muster, and the cricketing world of the 1950s was happy to accept them as such. In contrast, the same cannot be said for the other amateurs in the first-class game at the time. In fact, even in the 1930s it had been noted that there were only a few true amateurs. By the 1950s most were employed in jobs which allowed time off for cricket – teaching, public relations or as officials of county clubs. Not only were they accused of being 'shamateurs' but they were also just as aggressive as professionals in the game, and just as ruthless.

The favoured job was as county Secretary or Assistant Secretary. Trevor Bailey for Essex, Wilfred Wooller for Glamorgan, Raman Subba Row for Northamptonshire, Mike Smith for Warwickshire, Charles Palmer for Leicestershire, Donald Carr for Derbyshire, Peter Richardson for Worcestershire and Desmond Eagar for Hampshire were all in post in the middle 1950s. To be honest, they were none of them expected to do much secretarial work. Their job was to play cricket. Similarly, there were companies which for one reason or another felt it desirable to have amateur cricketers as token employees. Gunn and Moore, the manufacturers of cricket bats, Wimpey, the construction company, British Timken, the makers of ball bearings, and Sun Life, the insurers, had deals with Reg Simpson, Doug Insole, Freddie Brown (and at least half the Northamptonshire side) and Bob Wyatt respectively, while John Warr and Peter May himself found their livelihood provided by firms in the City of London.

These, however, were in the top rank of amateur cricketers. Just below them was another rank of mainly club players who flitted in and out of the county championship as occasion demanded and availability permitted. In 1954, for instance, of the five amateurs recorded as playing for Derbyshire only one – the captain (and county club Secretary) Donald Carr – played more than six out of thirty games. The score in Essex is less dramatic but similar. J. A. Bailey, T. E. Bailey and D. J. Insole all played a full season in the same year, but the only other amateur who mustered more than five games in the championship was C. C. P. Williams with nine – all of them after the end of the University season.

This gave some of those sides who depended relatively heavily on amateurs, Essex, Hampshire, Middlesex and Somerset, the tone of club cricket. Hampshire, in particular, under the captaincy of Colin Ingleby-Mackenzie, and Middlesex under the captaincy of John Warr, adopted an almost flippant approach to the game. It was much appreciated by senior figures in the MCC who thought it quintessentially the way amateurs should play cricket. Declarations in the third innings, for instance, should give opponents a chance of winning the match – and at the same time making them force the pace at the risk of losing wickets and so losing the game. Yet this was far from typical. Most county sides played to win or, if they could not win, at least not to lose.

In fact, during the 1950s there was an identifiable move by amateur captains away from what was perceived as the 'amateur' approach. In some measure it was a generational shift. The most dramatic example of the shift came in the MCC tour of the West Indies in 1959–60. Walter Robins, the traditionalist amateur, did his utmost to persuade the captain and vice-captain, Peter May and Colin Cowdrey, to use slow leg spin as a key element in the England bowling attack (the West Indian attack was reliant on pace) and to make sporting declarations in Test matches. Neither May nor Cowdrey, both of whom had played with and under professional captains who would never hear of such nonsense, agreed. Matters came to a head in the final Test when Cowdrey (May having withdrawn because of illness) honoured an agreement he had made with May and refused to make a declaration – telling his batsmen to bat out the game. This they did, drawing the match and winning the series. Robins then gave Cowdrey – in the dressing room and in front of the whole England team – a loud and very public dressing down. Since Robins was due to become Chairman of the England selectors Cowdrey realised that his chances of being given the captaincy in May's absence in the future were negligible.

Yet whatever the generational differences there is no doubt that the hardening of the amateur attitudes in cricket reflected the spirit of the times. Those of us who were aware of such things could see that by the middle of the decade the social and political climate had started

to change. Gone was the optimism of the early 1950s –
Britain victorious in war, the new Elizabethan age, the
conquest of Everest, the return of a Tory government
under Winston Churchill and the gradual relaxation of
post-war austerity. The whole return to the perceived
normalcy of the pre-war years had turned out to be a
chimera. The newer universities ('red-brick' they were
called) had started to assert themselves. It was the time
of *Lucky Jim* and *Look Back in Anger*, of the attack on
what later became called the 'Establishment'. The target,
it need hardly be said, was primarily old-school amateurs,
not least those who had been the 'gentlemen' of Victorian
and Edwardian England, who had commanded the British
armed forces through successive World Wars, and who
had run cricket – not just domestic cricket but international cricket – through the mechanism of their private
club, the MCC.

Many of those attacks could be shrugged off as com-
plaints by those who felt hard done by and could safely
be ignored. But the political turning point came in the
autumn of 1956 with the attack on Egypt in response to
the nationalisation of the Suez Canal. Not only was the
operation managed with outstanding military inefficiency
but the 'gentlemen' in charge of the British government at
the time were shown not just to be incompetent but liars
– and liars, as it happened, to the House of Commons.
Those of us who were alive at the time – and some of
us who were in our National Service in those months –
recall vividly the humiliation that the 'gentlemen' had
brought on Britain. It was no longer possible to maintain
that they were our natural leaders. True, there was a new

government under an Etonian, Harold Macmillan, and a group of 'gentlemen', but it would not be long before that, too, would begin to disintegrate in a flurry of sexual scandals.

The social turning point came with the abolition of National Service as the 1950s approached their close. On the cricket field the Combined Services during the days of universal conscription could put out a powerful side, full of eighteen- or nineteen-year-olds, many of whom either had played or would go on to play for their counties, and some of whom had already made their mark for England. They did not take kindly to being ordered about by inferior players just by virtue of rank. A prime example was the Combined Services match against the Australians in September 1953. Aircraftsman F. S. Trueman made it perfectly clear that he was not in the least interested in the cricket (Keith Miller and Jim de Courcy put on 377 for the fourth Australian wicket) by sitting on the sightscreen for much of the time. When reproved by an air vice-marshal after the game, Trueman gave an insolent answer. The furious air vice-marshal promptly told him that he would never play for the Combined Services again. 'Too bloody right,' Trueman replied. 'I'm being demobbed tomorrow.' Nevertheless, those who played in the Combined Services sides remember that they were both effective and competitive up to first-class standard. Moreover, leaving aside the intervention of clumsy senior officers, they narrowed the difference between those who were destined to be amateurs (officers) and those who were destined to be professionals (other ranks). We were all, whatever our rank, cricketers in common. It was a taste of what was to come. Leadership by the 'gentlemen' was no longer taken for granted.

3

THE PLAYERS

Player: one who is practised or skilled
at some game (OED)

One of the privileges offered to a cricketing Westminster schoolboy in the late 1940s was permission from time to time for an afternoon off to watch cricket at its highest – and for the schoolboy unattainable – level. Carefully selected, we could go, we were told on the most detailed instruction, either to the Oval or to Lord's – and, for obvious reasons, nowhere else (at least not to Soho). The adventure was, for us, something near to magic. Denis Compton and Bill Edrich in their pomp of 1947, Don Bradman in 1948 (alas, I saw him play only one stroke – just after I arrived, c Hutton b Bedser in the second innings of the Lord's Test for 38), all at Lord's, Len Hutton's 202 not out against the West Indian spinners Sonny Ramadhin and Alf Valentine in 1950 at the Oval, all are treasured memories of at least one wide-eyed schoolboy.

The English batsmen – professional as well as amateur – stood up to all we expected of them. The English bowlers, on the other hand (all professional apart from

Trevor Bailey), even to the young eye seemed very much less impressive – apart from Alec Bedser, bowling fast-medium inswingers and, when the wet wickets favoured it, a formidable leg cutter. Bedser certainly had some notable scalps, and Don Bradman himself thought him one of the greatest bowlers he had played against, but it was a revelation to see the Australian bowlers of 1948, Ray Lindwall and Keith Miller, bowling at fast but controlled pace with, in Lindwall's case, the ability to swing the ball away from the bat and, in Miller's, to pitch the ball on the seam with – for the batsman – unpredictable movements. We, the schoolboys, had seen nothing like it before.

It was, after all, the 1940s and the war had only just ended. In fact, at the time the legacy of the war (and the ensuing Labour government) was blamed for everything which went wrong. That was true even in cricket. Some said that the long period of service in the armed forces had left the successors of the Larwood and Voce of the early 1930s without the muscles for fast bowling (although the Australian bowlers of the day seemed to have survived without difficulty). Some also said that the years of wartime aggression devoted to attacking a common enemy had blunted the hostile edge of those who had survived. Others, mainly older members of the MCC, lamented the demise of a whole generation and thought that, particularly with Labour in power, things would never be the same again.

Those were, of course, extreme views. Nevertheless, there was still a point. Those of us who qualified as callow schoolboys at an early age for 'playing membership' of the MCC noted that we could with one telephone call arrange for the young professionals on the staff to come out at short notice and bowl at us in the Lord's nets. Their task done, there was no further communication and they went quietly back to their own dressing rooms. That was, to the concerned observer, the inglorious side of professional cricket.

Even so, there is no doubt that the war and its aftermath marked a definitive, and, as it turned out, irreversible change in the status of the professional cricketer. In 1949, at the instigation of the then President, the Duke of Edinburgh, twenty-six former England professional players were made honorary life members of the hitherto gentlemanly (and amateur) MCC. In 1951 a professional, Tom Dollery, was not only appointed captain of Warwickshire but led his county to win the championship. By then most counties had phased out the use of separate dressing rooms for amateurs and professionals (the Oval being the notable exception) and the practice of emerging on to the playing field from separate gates. In 1953, Jack Hobbs was given a knighthood (much to his embarrassment – he asked the President of Surrey, Sir Walter Monckton, to use his influence to cancel the appointment). Finally, in the same year, Len Hutton was asked to captain England against Australia in the Ashes series (although he was invited to turn amateur for the purpose but resolutely refused to do so).

As the status of the professional improved, so did the numbers in the first-class game. In 1929, for instance, no fewer than 205 amateurs had played in the county championship. By 1959 that figure had dwindled to thirty-nine, over half of whom played fewer than ten matches. The professionals, as a matter of course, took up the slack. Furthermore, there was more movement of personnel between counties. In 1944 the MCC sanctioned a procedure entitled 'special registration'. Under its provisions, counties were allowed to apply to register players from other counties who were not required either by the county of their residence or by the county of their birth without obliging them to complete the customary year's residence in their new county. In 1953 the provisions were tightened to two such transfers in any one year and a maximum of ten specially registered players at any one time. Moreover, the MCC set up a special committee to monitor the system – and to approve or disapprove registrations. In fact, the committee did disapprove three applicants between 1956 and 1961, Mike Smith (an amateur) wishing to move from Leicestershire to Warwickshire, Peter Richardson (also an amateur) from Worcestershire to Kent and Tom Graveney (a professional) from Gloucestershire to Worcestershire. (The special registration of C. C. P. Williams in 1953 for transfer from Oxfordshire to Essex, where my mother had taken up residence, thankfully passed without a murmur.)

Although this marked a relaxation of the former strict policy of qualification solely by birth or residence, it still did not put cricketers on any sort of par with other professions. A teacher or an architect, for instance, if he or she disliked his or her present position, was free to move elsewhere (subject, of course, to any contractual complications). A cricketer would still be bound by residence or birth qualifications even under the new system of special registration – unless he could get the approval to move to another from what was, after all, no more than an un-elected committee of a private members' club.

In practice, special registrations were infrequent, which was as it was meant to be and why the scheme was en-titled 'special'. Most cricketers stayed to play for the first county for which they qualified. Yorkshire, for instance, had a very strict policy of qualification by birth – and in fact was one of the counties which exported most play-ers to others (in the 1950s Essex had three Yorkshiremen as regular members of the first eleven). But there was also a strong sense of loyalty to a county (particularly Yorkshire, even among its expatriates). The two profes-sional batting stars of the period for instance, Hutton and Compton, remained with their initial counties, Yorkshire and Middlesex respectively, for the whole of their careers.

In fact, Len Hutton was very much a case in point. He would never have even thought about leaving Yorkshire. Born and growing up on the Fulneck estate in Pudsey, a village then on the edge of Leeds but which has now been subsumed into the city itself, he was the quintes-sential Yorkshireman. But there was more to it than Yorkshire. Fulneck was, and is, the site of the founda-tion in 1744 by Count Nicolaus Ludwig von Zinzendorf, himself a Lutheran bishop from Bohemia, of a branch of the Moravian Church. The name of the community was originally 'Lamb's Hill', a name derived from the Book of Revelation. But the name, apparently, did not catch on and in the middle of the nineteenth century it was changed to Fulneck – in honour of Bishop John Comenius who had ministered to the faithful in Fulnek, Moravia. As Len Hutton learnt in his early years, the Moravian Christians were devoted to their own particular faith, puritan and (very) strait-laced. It was an unlikely origin for one of the greatest batsmen England has ever produced.

And it certainly left its mark. To meet, Hutton was reserved, taciturn and, on occasions, caustic. To talk to he could be full of smiles, but behind the smiles there was a detectable realm of silence. There were secrets which could not be revealed. Nevertheless, he realised that he had a particular talent (he thought of it in the biblical terms of the Parable of the Talents) and applied his talent to cricket. Even at the age of sixteen he was playing regularly in the Bradford Cricket League. At the age of seventeen, in 1934, he made his first appearance for Yorkshire (run out for nought in his first innings) and in 1937 he played his first Test match for England against New Zealand (unsuccessfully – out for nought in the first innings and one in the second). Yet even at the start of his career, and in spite of a rather twisted Moravian education, he showed a clear ability to think about the game, and its subtleties (a characteristic which was not always evident in his fellow professionals or, indeed, in many amateurs).

Hutton was ambitious, even at the expense of his colleagues. An early example of dedicated selfishness was the Gentlemen vs Players match at Lord's of 1938. Ken Farnes, the amateur Essex fast bowler, had been dropped from the England Test side, and was thus in a particularly bad mood, and when Farnes was in a bad mood he bowled very fast. Hutton and Bill Edrich opened the batting for the Players, Hutton signalling straightaway to Edrich that he should take Farnes's first ball. It was fast and furious and rose steeply – Farnes was powerfully built and was six foot four tall – but wide. The second ball touched Edrich's glove and ricocheted to hit him between the eyes, laying him out. When he regained consciousness, Edrich staggered back to the crease only to find that gully had caught the ball off his head and, on appeal, that he had been given out. Hutton, at the bowler's end, showed little sympathy. He was, after all, still not out.

It was not the only occasion where Hutton was demonstrably selfish. In the 1948 season, against the fierce speed of Lindwall and Miller, it was generally remarked (not least by Bradman) how often Hutton, if required to face the first over of an England innings, managed almost imperceptibly to take a single off the first or second ball and stay at the bowler's end for the rest of the over. To be fair, Hutton himself used sometimes to joke about it. When asked the best way to play Lindwall and Miller he replied 'from the bowler's end'. It was his way of saying, in true Yorkshire fashion, that you did not play the game for fun.

Technically, Hutton's batting was almost immaculate. His grip on the bat – both wrists turned behind the handle to allow the face of the bat to close when playing on the on side – was surprisingly similar to Bradman's. They were, of course, wholly different in style and temperament. Where Bradman was ruthless and aggressive Hutton was cautious and defensive. Bradman's trademark was the pull shot, Hutton's the push to leg. Both, however, were aware that the grip also allowed the bat to be closed when playing the cut shot, thus running the ball safely along the ground. Where both were truly remarkable was in their ability, in spite of the limitations of the grip, to play the cover drive with great beauty.

Hutton, again like Bradman, had a difficult Second World War. After successful seasons in 1937 (scoring 2,888 runs in first-class cricket), 1938 (achieving the Test record of 364 in just over thirteen hours, the longest innings in first-class cricket at the time) and 1939 (averaging 96.00 in Test matches against the West Indies), he volunteered for the Army at the outset of war and was drafted into the Army Physical Training Corps. As sergeant-instructor he was posted to the commando training centre in York, so that during 1940 he was able to play cricket in the charity matches then being organised.

In March 1941 he had a serious accident. In the training centre gym a mat slipped from under him and he fell on his left arm, breaking his forearm and dislocating his left wrist. The operation to secure his arm seemed to have been a success since he returned to his job in the summer. But the pain would not subside. In fact it became worse. Two further operations were attempted, to graft bone from his leg into his arm. Although it was claimed that the second was successful, he came out with his left arm two inches shorter than his right. In the middle of 1942 he was therefore discharged from the Army and spent the rest of the war as a civilian inspector of damaged buildings – and playing cricket for Pudsey St Lawrence in the Bradford League.

The injury and its after-effects in the end made him change his batting style. He was hit twice on the damaged arm by Keith Miller, in 1944 and later in the second Test of the Ashes tour of 1946–7. Both blows were very painful. Not only did he become more cautious when facing the faster bowlers (particularly Miller) but also, since he found it difficult to rotate his left wrist anticlockwise, he was obliged to cut out the hook shot. Scenting a weakness, Lindwall and Miller bowled fast and short. In return, Hutton adopted the technique of ducking under the bouncers – which in turn led the Australian press to assert roundly that he was 'yellow'.

Whatever the truth of the accusation, he was certainly in poor health in 1947 and 1948 – he had developed tonsillitis in early 1947, had asked to be left out of the MCC side to tour the West Indies in 1947–8 and looked, to those of us who were watching the 1948 Lord's Test sitting on the grass in front of the Tavern, pale and distracted. He was also batting badly and – horror of horrors – seemed to be backing away from Lindwall and Miller. After scoring an uncomfortable 20 and 13, he walked back to the pavilion at the end of his second innings to total silence. We guessed what was coming: he was dropped for the third Test. Recalled for the fourth Test at Headingley, he redeemed himself by making 81 and 57. Oddly, he was even required by the then captain Norman Yardley to bowl during the hectic Australian last innings (Australia scored 404 in the day to win the match; Hutton bowled four overs for thirty runs).

By the turn of the decade Hutton had established himself, in the opinion of both *Wisden* and the Australian press, as the best batsman in the world (Bradman having by then retired). A Sydney firm gave him £1,000 as the best player in the 1950–51 series, in which he averaged 88.83. In the English season of 1951 he scored his hundredth first-class century, was appointed captain of England in 1952 and won the Ashes for England in 1953 for the first time since 1932–3 (it was the first home series win since 1926). He missed a large part of the 1954 season through ill health but returned to captain England again in the successful Ashes tour of 1954–5.

It was the true highlight of his career and it was recognised as such. On his return he was made an honorary member of the MCC, but again succumbed to ill health and could not play in the 1955 season after June. In January 1956 he announced his retirement and in the 1956 Birthday Honours he was awarded a knighthood.

Those of us who watched Hutton – particularly his innings in 1950 against Ramadhin and Valentine on a rain-affected wicket – were in no doubt that we were watching a truly exceptional player. Some called it genius, some just extraordinary intuition. Of course, his great strength lay in his defensive technique, playing the ball as late as possible and watching closely on to his bat; if he can be criticised, it might be said that he was indeed too defensive, and so too cautious.

The same could not be said of the other outstanding professional batsman of the time, Denis Compton. In character, temperament and style he was almost the direct opposite to Hutton. For a start he was a southerner, born and bred in the London suburb of Hendon in 1918, the year the First World War ended. Moreover, he was also a genuinely all-round athlete, not just a batsman and bowler of left-arm wrist spin in cricket but a footballer of skill, winning the FA Cup with Arsenal in 1950. Compton, like Hutton, was a product of the elementary education of the time. There was no point in trying to go on to university, although he was intelligent enough. His parents could not have afforded it even if they had thought it worth a try. The career path for a young man of his class in the 1930s was simple: if possible, and whatever the difficulties, find a job – and never let it go voluntarily since you might never find another one. Fortunately, Compton discovered that he had one precious asset – something touching genius in his eye. At sixteen he was accepted for a post on the MCC ground staff and thereafter – never letting a job go voluntarily – played for Middlesex throughout his career.

As with both Hutton and Bradman, Compton's career was interrupted by the Second World War. He volunteered for the Army and, unlike them, served throughout the war, for the most of it in India. There he was, by all reports, not only in cricketing demand but in social demand as well (not least, as it turned out, from women). There were many stories of his flamboyance and general *joie de vivre*. On one occasion, for instance, he is said to have quelled a mob which had invaded the pitch during a match at Eden Gardens in Calcutta while he was batting by producing a packet of cigarettes from his back pocket and offering them all round. Only 'Compo', it was said, would have gone out to bat with a packet of cigarettes in his back pocket.

Even in the wartime India, Compton saw no reason to stop enjoying himself. He made friends with Keith Miller – the friendship was to last their lifetimes – and their drinking bouts were so heavy and prolonged that even the Viceroy's office took sad note. The pattern continued after the war, only by that time the preferred drinking (and batting) partner, although not the only one, was Bill Edrich. By that time, Compton was the star of the series of advertisements for the men's hair lotion Brylcreem which brought him £5,000 a year and an army of adoring women (he was forced to recruit an agent to deal with the fan mail). None of this, of course, changed his enthusiastic lifestyle – drinking, betting on horses, women coming and going, practical joking – which caused a good number of heads in the Middlesex establishment and the MCC to frown in disapproval.

Flamboyance and enjoyment continued to be Compton's theme in the decade after the end of the war. At times, in fact, they toppled over into indiscipline. And on one occasion, he forgot to turn up for the last day of practice before a Lord's Test against the Australians and had to be told that if he did that again he would be dropped for the final Test at the Oval. He covered up during the Australian tour of 1946–7 for Edrich who had failed to return after one of his all-night binges; Compton explained to his captain, Hammond – with a straight face – that Edrich had just slipped out to buy some oysters for breakfast. He turned up for the Old Trafford Test of 1955 against South Africa without his kitbag (he found an old bat in the neighbouring museum, borrowed it and went out to make 155 and 74 not out). And in his brother Leslie's benefit he managed to run the beneficiary out before he had faced a ball.

Yet for all his eccentricities, Compton as a batsman was a joy to watch. Unlike Hutton, he was forever experimenting with novel shots. The result was that when he was sparking no bowler knew where to bowl to him. In spite of a series of operations on a knee which had been badly damaged in football he was nimble enough when he wished to be – until in 1958 he found that the knee could not be relied on and he retired from the first-class game, after scoring 123 centuries.

Although Hutton and Compton were the brightest in the firmament, there were many other professionals who, on their day, could match them. Cyril Washbrook of Lancashire, Ken Barrington of Surrey, Willie Watson of Yorkshire, Tom Graveney of Gloucestershire, Bill Edrich of Middlesex, Don Kenyon of Worcestershire and Jim Parks of Sussex were all effective and (particularly so in Graveney's case) elegant. There were, of course, the journeymen batsmen as well – those who were determined not to get out to the point where they omitted to play any strokes (they were the ones we dreaded fielding against – toiling uncomfortably as they scratched away for their runs). There were also batsmen of the second rank – good but not quite up to Test standard. Yet, all in all, by the mid-1950s the professionals could put out batting sides in every county which matched the amateur stars of the day.

The improvement in professionals' batting in the ten years after the end of the war was more than matched by the improvement in their bowling. In fact, by the mid-1950s a truly formidable team of bowlers had emerged to form the attack for their counties and England: Frank Tyson, Brian Statham, Fred Trueman, Peter Loader, Alec Bedser, Jim Laker, Tony Lock and Johnny Wardle. They were all fine bowlers, but if they are to be ranked by speed there is no doubt that Tyson led the pack.

Tyson was born in Bolton in 1930 to middle-class parents. Educated at Middleton Grammar School, he went on to study English at the University of Durham and to qualify as a teacher. As such, he was an unusual professional (very few had been through higher education) and, although he never lost his Lancashire accent, seemed to regard himself as being a cut, or even a cut and a half, above his colleagues. In fact, although normally good-tempered, he had bursts of anger – some of it from time to time directed at amateurs, but if he liked you he could be quite charming. For instance, for those batsmen he disliked (he had a particular animus towards Ray Lindwall) his language was robust; but for those he liked he would, when they missed a ball (as frequently happened), he was given to staring hard at them and quoting Wordsworth: 'For still, the more he works the more do his weak ankles swell.' It was particularly unnerving.

Tall, and with a rather thin, gangling figure, Tyson looked an unlikely candidate for the title of one of the fastest, if not *the* fastest, bowlers who ever bowled a cricket ball. When he made his debut for Northamptonshire (after transfer from Lancashire on special registration), his first ball was so quick that the wicketkeeper and slips immediately moved back five yards. Against the 1953 Australians, who had been assured that they had nothing to worry about, Tyson took two wickets in his first over, the second a clean hit which sent the batsman's off stump flying over the wicketkeeper's head. He followed this in 1954 by breaking Bill Edrich's jaw at Lord's and, at Old Trafford on a rain-affected wicket, to general astonishment a bouncer reared up and smashed into the sight-screen without any further contact with the ground. He was, understandably, forthwith selected for the 1954–5

MCC tour of Australia. Once there, after a failure in the first Test, he shortened his run and, with Statham, bowled England to victory in three of the following four Tests.

In those days, when wickets were uncovered and there were no helmets, it was difficult for those without the eye to pick up the flight of the ball very early (a category which in practice was mostly limited to Test batsmen) to play Tyson. It was unwise to move forward since the ball could rear alarmingly off a length. But it was also unwise to move backwards since there was always the risk of a yorker or lbw if the ball skidded. The only way to play him was to move slightly backwards (nowadays it is called the 'trigger' movement) and be ready to shift the body weight forward for a ball of a good length or fuller and back for a shorter ball while carefully preparing to duck a bouncer. If the ball was full it could be pushed in front of the wicket and if it was shorter it could be played off the hip. In all this the batsman had two advantages. First, Tyson never moved the ball. Unlike Lindwall, he never mastered the technique; the ball came fast – but straight. Second, the speed of the ball made playing shots unnecessary. A push or a steer through gully would easily go to the boundary using Tyson's own speed.

In 1960 Tyson retired from first-class cricket and moved to Australia, following his hero, Harold Larwood. He left his 1954–5 bowling partner, Brian Statham. to stay in England. That, of course, was not the only difference between the two. Statham (he collected the nickname 'George' apparently because there were no players in the Lancashire side with that name but plenty of Brians) was in character almost the opposite of the volcanic Tyson.

He, too, was a Lancastrian, born in Manchester in June 1930, four days, as it happened, after Tyson himself. His parents were poor and there was no question of higher education. In fact there was little education at all – and certainly no cricket coaching. Leaving school at fourteen, he immediately signed up to a crickcting career, first for Stockport in the Central Lancashire League, then, during his National Service, for RAF teams in Stafford where he was based and, in 1949, for Lancashire.

Statham took a long time to emerge into the cricket limelight. Apart from all else, the pitches at Old Trafford in his early years were more favourable to the Lancashire spin bowlers Roy Tattersall and Malcolm Hilton than they were to pace. Furthermore, Statham was no quicker than fast medium. During 1950 and 1951, however, he modified his bowling action to become genuinely fast (although never quite as fast as Tyson). In addition, he mastered the technique of landing the ball on the seam in a way which allowed a fast deviation off the wicket and into the off stump. This made it impossible for batsmen to play him the way they could play Tyson. It was one thing playing from the crease to Tyson, when the ball did not deviate either in thc air or off the wicket. It was a quite different thing to try to play Statham in thc samc manner. The risk of allowing the ball to complete its movement off the seam was too great (Statham's victims wcre very often either clean-bowled or lbw). Fortunately, the batsman had a compensating advantage: Statham's action, although orthodox, tended to make the ball skid rather than kick. Playing forward was therefore possible without danger. Besides, he very rarely bowled a bouncer (and often warned the batsman when he was going to do so). Furthermore, his consistency of length and line, although it made it difficult to score, made him from time to time and on good wickets rather predictable.

In 1950 Statham was selected for the England Test side, but he could never be sure of a place. After a poor series in India in 1951–2 he was dropped altogether for 1952 and was lucky to be called up during the Ashes Test series of 1953, although in the event he did not get a game. He was, however, selected for the MCC tour of the West Indies in 1953–4 and it was there that he made his name, bowling fast and accurately on mostly flat wickets. He performed well against the Pakistanis in 1954 and was an obvious selection for the Ashes tour of 1954–5. There, in partnership with Tyson (Trueman had been dropped after the West Indies tour) he did exactly what was required of him. Tyson was to be the strike bowler, Statham, always bowling into the wind to allow Tyson maximum speed, ensured that the Australian batsmen would know no peace.

Tyson came back from Australia with a blistered heel. That, and a drop in his form on English wickets, allowed Trueman to come back as Statham's partner for England. From 1955 to 1963 they bowled as a pair. During the Ashes tour of 1962–3 Statham broke the Test record of 236 wickets during the fourth Test in Adelaide, taking his total to 242 – but only held it for two months when Trueman went further. After that Statham never quite reached his earlier heights again, although by others' standards he was still a master bowler. He finally retired in 1968, at which point he was awarded a CBE. In the citation it was noted that his first-class bowling average of 16.37 was the lowest of any bowler since 1900 who had taken 2,000 first-class wickets.

Statham's partner in the England attack after Tyson's retirement was Fred Trueman, a true son of Yorkshire, described by no less than Prime Minister Harold Wilson as 'the greatest living Yorkshireman'. It therefore comes as something of a surprise to find the name of Frederick Sewards Trueman on the list of Jewish cricketers. In fact, it was not until late in his life that Trueman discovered that his maternal grandmother was Jewish. On being told of this, and of the fact that Jewish custom and law would recognise him as Jewish, he replied, diplomatically, that he was happy to be called Jewish.

Such diplomacy was for his later years. In his earlier years, Trueman was a Yorkshire tearaway. Born in 1931 in the village of Stainton in the West Riding of Yorkshire, he passed secondary school in Maltby. During the war he took a number of jobs – builder's mate, apprentice in a wire works and then in a glass factory; in spite of the sub-sequent mythology, Trueman was never a miner – he did a winter job as a tally clerk at Maltby Main Colliery in an effort to avoid National Service, only to find that the job was removed from the list of 'reserved occupations' and that he would be called up nonetheless. At the end of the war, he was playing cricket for Sheffield United's second team, bowling fast and mostly inaccurately, to the point where he was invited, in 1948 and at the age of sixteen, to join the Yorkshire Federation team, the county side for players under eighteen. What Trueman had, and which attracted the Yorkshire selectors, was the ability to swing the ball away from the bat at speed. With his big shoulders and hips and strong legs, and a long, looping run-up to the wicket, he was able to turn side-on, raise his left arm at the same time as stretching his right behind and so bowl the perfect cartwheel for the outswinger. Lindwall was the master of the art. Yorkshire, and subsequently England, thought that they had their riposte.

Trueman duly did his National Service from 1951 to 1953 at the Royal Air Force base at Hemswell in Lincolnshire. In truth, it was hardly more than a token air force career – if even that. He was summoned to play for the RAF against the Army and the Navy, for the Combined Services in sporadic matches against the Public Schools and the odd county side, and in 1952 he was given leave to play nine first-class matches, of which five were Tests against India. (His Test debut against India was spectacular: he immediately took three wickets without conceding a run.)

Trueman was demobilised at the beginning of the 1953 winter, just in time to tour the West Indies in 1953–4. It promised well but turned out to be an altogether unhappy experience. He did not get on with the captain, Hutton, whom he thought to be a social climber. Neither did he get on well with the Chairman of selectors, G. O. ('Gubby') Allen, whom he thought (rightly) to be an inveterate snob. Nor, in fact, did he like the other amateurs much – they were all, underneath their veneer of talent, at bottom just 'fancy caps'. Furthermore, the West Indian crowds took against him, not least because of his aggressive attitude on the field and his refusal to apologise to a batsman who had just been hit. Both on and off the field he was gauche and frequently simply racist (at a dinner party he is said to have addressed the Indian High Commissioner as 'Gunga Din'; the following day, while fielding on the boundary, he was so incensed by the barrage of heckling that he turned round and invited the hecklers in a loud voice to go back up the tree where their fathers had come from). As a result, unsurprisingly but much to his fury, his good-conduct bonus was docked and subsequently Hutton made sure that Trueman was left out of the England side for all the Tests against Pakistan in 1954 and the Ashes tour of 1954–5.

It was not until 1957 (and Hutton's retirement) that Trueman was able to reclaim his place in the England team. In that year he played in all five Tests against the West Indies and so began his six-year partnership with Statham as the spearhead of the attack – Trueman fast, unpredictable but always a dynamic force, Statham fast, accurate and persistent. Almost always in partner-ship with Statham, Trueman played in all Tests in 1957, 1958, on the Ashes tour of 1958–9, in 1959, on the West Indies tour of 1959–60, in 1960, in 1961 (but missing the last Test through injury), 1962 (again missing the last Test), on the Ashes tour of 1962–3, 1963, 1964 (when he became the first bowler to take 300 Test wickets) and 1965. He finished his Test career in that year, with 307 wickets at an average of 21.54.

Whatever else he did, good or bad, Trueman at least brought character to the game. Although he took his bowling very seriously, he was never short of a word and, at least on occasions, a joke. When he was batting or field-ing (he was a brilliant in-fielder) he was sometimes able to keep a crowd laughing long and loud at his antics. For those who played against him he was always difficult to deal with when his outswinger was working (again there was no question of playing him like Tyson unless it was for catching practice in the slips) and he was quite ready, as an added bonus, to let the batsman know his opinion at full volume if he had played and missed. Nevertheless, at least one who played against him (the author) came away with the impression that at heart Trueman was a generous soul, and because of that he was not terrifying. Frightening, yes, but not terrifying.

The same could not be said of the fourth member of the England fast-bowling quartet of the mid-1950s, Peter Loader. Loader never made any effort, on or off the field, to get on with batsmen, whether amateur or professional. He was venomous both in the way he bowled and in his abuse of the batsman at whom he was bowling. At times his colleagues had to restrain him since he frequently lost his temper – at which point he was liable to lose his bowling action and spray his deliveries anywhere between first slip and leg slip, thus allowing the batsman to laugh at him, which inflamed him, as was intended, still more.

There was also no doubt in our minds, nor in those of some of his county colleagues (and Frank Tyson), that he threw his bouncer, as well as his slower off cutter. Those who faced the bouncer knew full well that there was a moment – a microsecond – when the batsman suddenly realised that Loader was going to bowl from wide on the crease. It was his preferred place from which to throw his bouncer. As it happened, it was also his preferred place for delivery (with a legal action) of an outswinging yorker. The batsman then had to make a choice – given that the ball was coming at him at between eighty and ninety miles an hour. Early in the ball's flight he had to decide which one it was going to be. The wrong decision was likely to be fatal, in one sense or another. If he had decided it was to be a bouncer and it turned out to be a yorker, delivered at Loader's normal pace, he would be starting to duck and almost certainly be out lbw. Equally, if he decided it was to be a yorker and it turned out to be a bouncer, delivered at exceptional pace, he risked – literally, in the days before helmets – near decapitation. It was always, on either option, hazardous in one way or another. But at least with the yorker the batsman would escape with his skin. With the bouncer it was life-threatening – and the only way to play it was to duck into the flight of the ball rather than away from it, since, if the batsman tried to sway away from it, the ball, because of the angle, would follow his head. Whatever the result, the batsman could be sure of receiving from Loader a torrent of unpleasant, even vitriolic, abuse.

Yet Loader had a particular talent. He was able to swing the new ball away from the bat at pace – and late – from whatever angle on the crease he chose to bowl. He was particularly destructive on the hard wickets of the Oval. But his favourite moment was to bowl at the opening batsmen of an opposing county side after they had been in the field almost all the day. In those moments, unpleasant as he was, Loader had his times of near genius.

There was nothing in Loader's personal history that gives any clue to his erratic temperament. He was born in 1929 in the benign London suburb of Wallington into a benign middle-class family and, although troubled by asthma, decided, after secondary education at Beddington School, to train as a dental mechanic. He joined Beddington Cricket Club as a boy determined to bowl fast in spite of his slender physique. Picked up by Surrey County Cricket Club in 1951, he was invited to play, first as an amateur and then, from 1952 onwards, on the professional staff. For the next ten years he was an automatic choice for Surrey when he was fit.

Loader's Test career depended on the availability of Tyson, Statham and Trueman. His first Test was the fourth against Pakistan in 1954, but, although he went on the Ashes tour of 1954–5 and did well in the State games, he was not picked for another Test until the fourth against South Africa in 1955. There was a further tour of South Africa in 1956–7 with four further Tests and, finally, the Ashes tour of 1958–9. Although that marked the end of his Test career, Loader continued to play for Surrey to great effect. It was not until 1962 that he decided to retire and emigrate to Western Australia (where he ran a taxi business).

A much more pleasant character was Alec Bedser. He was the warhorse who carried the England bowling immediately after the war. He and his twin brother Eric were born in 1918 and grew up in Horsell in Surrey. They were, throughout their lives, inseparable. They were also almost indistinguishable one from the other, not least because they dressed always alike – the same suit, the same tie, the same shirt, the same shoes; they even had the same way of speaking. (We all of us at some point, at least once and some more than once, thought that we were addressing Alec when in fact it was Eric. They thought it a great, if slightly ponderous, joke.)

The two Bedsers started training with a firm of local solicitors but were recruited to the Surrey staff in 1938. The following year they made their first appearance in a first-class game for Surrey at the Oval. Almost immediately, however, war broke out and they volunteered for the Royal Air Force. They managed (nobody quite knows how) to stay together during the war, notably in the evacuation at Dunkirk and in the North African and Italian campaigns.

Demobilised in 1946, the Bedsers settled down again to professional cricket, Alec bowling medium fast – typically inswingers – and Eric bowling off spin. Both of them could perform well with the bat as well (but were horribly bad fielders). Alec took 100 wickets in county games by the end of June 1946 and was an obvious choice for England's Ashes tour of 1946–7. Thereafter he was a fixture in the England side until the Ashes tour of 1954–5 when, in the first Test, suffering from a bad attack of shingles, he took 1 for 131. Dropped from the Test side, apart from one game against South Africa in 1955, he played (as did Eric) devotedly for Surrey until his retirement in 1960. Thereafter, he became the nearest thing to a cricket grandee: twenty-three years as an England selector, twelve of which as Chairman, manager of two overseas tours, President of Surrey and, to crown it all, a knighthood in 1996.

From 1952 to 1953 until the late 1950s the top English professionals, together with the amateur Trevor Bailey, formed a pace attack which was the best in the world at the time. Nor were their spin bowler colleagues backward. They were numerous but, of all of them, Jim Laker is nowadays perhaps the best known. Originally from Bradford in Yorkshire, Laker settled in 1945, at the age of twenty-three, in the south London suburbs. Rejected by Yorkshire, he applied for special registration to join Surrey and by 1947 was playing for England. Between 1948 and 1959 he played in forty-six Tests taking, in all, 193 wickets, but certainly his finest performance was on a rain-affected wicket in the fourth Ashes Test at Old Trafford in 1956. His ability to spin the ball heavily from the off to the right-handed bat, deftly flighted but with the variation of a delivery going straight on, made him on that day and on that wicket unplayable – at least by the Australians. But he was a grumbler, and in his (ghost-written) autobiography of 1960 was so critical of the Surrey captain Peter May that he fell out of favour with Surrey and never played for them or England again.

Laker's bowling partner both for Surrey and England was the left-arm orthodox spinner Tony Lock. Lock was born at Limpsfield in Surrey in 1929 and was signed up by Surrey at the age of seventeen in 1946. His start was uncertain – at first he could not find a place in the Surrey side – but by 1949 he was playing regularly. His first call for England was against India in the third Test of 1952. Thereafter his performance was inconsistent: he was devastating on a wet wicket, spinning the ball away from the right-handed bat with venom but, because of his relatively fast pace, he was unable to flight the ball to deceive the batsman in the air, which put him at a disadvantage on the dry wickets of Australia. Yet he ended up with 174 Test wickets at an average 25.58.

These are the facts of Lock's career. But throughout it his bowling action was the subject of major controversy. On the surface, he seemed to be an orthodox left-arm finger spinner. There were, however, two deliveries by way of variation. One was a fast straight delivery (very fast, in fact) to take the batsman by surprise. The other was a heavily spun delivery with an almost round-arm action. Many thought that the faster ball was thrown, but on analysis Lock was cleared. His basic action, however, as well as the heavily spun ball, was with a bent elbow. Those who have tried know well that it is much easier to spin the ball hard by throwing than by bowling with a straight arm. Lock was called for throwing from time to time but nobody seemed to wish to take further action. The controversy rolled on until Lock looked at his action on film in 1961 – and promptly burst into tears. He realised then that he had been bowling illegally all along.

The third in the trio was Johnny Wardle. Wardle was born in Barnsley in Yorkshire into a mining family in 1923. During the war he played what club cricket there was in Yorkshire and from there was recruited to Yorkshire County Cricket Club. By 1950 he was playing on the fringes of the England side, where he remained for the whole of his career. Try as he might, he was unable to dislodge Lock from his preferred position as Laker's bowling partner, although he consistently took wickets for Yorkshire, and in the winter of 1956–7 so bemused the South African batsmen that he took twenty-six wickets in the series (7 for 36 in the second Test).

There are those, not all of them Yorkshiremen, who claim that Wardle was a better bowler than Lock. He was able to bowl orthodox left-arm spin when it suited and left-arm wrist spin on harder wickets. He was also consistently accurate and seemingly never tired. Yet he was in many respects a figure apart from others. When fielding or batting he often used to clown about (some of his antics were, in truth, extremely funny) but in the dressing room he was apt to be morose and – be it said – something of a troublemaker. He never got on with the members of the Yorkshire committee and was unwise enough in 1958 to write in the *Daily Mail* rubbishing the Yorkshire committee (in other words, his employers). He was immediately dropped and, on top of that, the MCC withdrew their invitation for the Ashes tour of 1958–9. When Wardle applied for a special registration to move to Nottinghamshire his application was brusquely turned down by the Yorkshire committee. He never played first-class cricket again.

Both in the counties and on overseas tours the professionals and the amateurs of the day, unlike those in other sports, lived and played alongside each other, albeit with varying degrees of tension between them. In fact, the England sides of the mid-1950s were arguably the strongest England sides of the twentieth century. Comparisons, of course, are difficult since the game has changed so much over the years. Nevertheless, simply to rehearse the achievements of the leading players – and to realise that underneath them in ability there were many, batsmen and bowlers, who in lean years would have filled an England place with honour – is to appreciate the strength in depth of the English game of the time. Attendances at county grounds were still good and the press coverage substantial and enthusiastic. There are those who talk of the golden age before the First World War. Perhaps it is time to recognise at least a silver age after the Second.

And yet, in spite of the successes on the field, all was not well. The structure of the game, the fuddy-duddy members of county committees, the arrogance of the MCC, the class system, the differential remuneration of amateurs and professionals, everything contributed to what perceptive observers termed a sense of unease. As it happened, much of the unease seemed to focus on the area where the amateur/professional divide was most obvious – the way the captains of counties and of England were chosen and how they were expected to act.

THE CAPTAINS

O Captain! My Captain! Our fearful trip is done

Before 1962 and the abolition of the distinction between amateur and professional, the two groups, with the exception of the Gentlemen vs Players matches, played on the same side. After 1962, of course, there was only one category of 'cricketer' and the distinction disappeared. There were, it need hardly be said, underlying tensions which might have led to serious friction, but, in practice, and in spite of all, relations between the two, at least in the 1950s, were reasonably good. There was, however, one open sore. It was the question of who should hold the captaincy of a county or indeed, most sensitive of all, of the England side.

Both history and – yet again – English class barriers played their part in the controversy. From the end of the nineteenth century it had been firmly established in the minds of those claiming to be in charge of events that only gentlemen were fit by nature to be leaders – and hence officers. Those who were not gentlemen had to be content with being 'other ranks'. In the light of the experience of

two World Wars, and the humiliating fiasco of the Suez
expedition in 1956, the doctrine, such as it was, came
under serious attack. But it took time for it to become
finally discredited. Until then cricket conformed to the
general principle: captains, like officers, should be gentlemen (hence amateurs) because they were the natural
leaders. Professionals, like other ranks, were by nature
labourers who were there to obey orders – and, of course,
to bow to their social superiors.

This general view had been stated most clearly by
the fearsome Lord Hawke, President of Yorkshire and
Treasurer of the MCC from 1932 to 1938. Lord Hawke
declared roundly, in 1925 at the annual general meeting
of the Yorkshire County Cricket Club, that on no account
should professionals – much as he admired them – ever
captain England. From then on the fault line developed
between those who supported Lord Hawke – including
almost all the members of the MCC – and the radicals in
the sporting press (and professionals in Yorkshire itself)
who felt that he was only talking from unreasoning class
prejudice.

In spite of the dissenting voices, the Hawke view domi-
nated cricket during the interwar period. As it happened,
at that time the fault line was for the most part quies
cent. After the Second World War, however, it started
to throw up some explosive verbal material. Len Hutton,
for instance, not known for public declarations, wrote sol-
emnly in 1956 that those who had received the King's
commission to lead their troops into battle were worthy of
the honour of leading England in cricket. Others – again
including members of the MCC with almost unanimous

voice – vociferously echoed the Hawke view. Leading the traditionalist charge were Gubby Allen and Walter Robins. Amateurism, they maintained, was the guarantee that the game should be played as it ought to be, in a spirit of gentlemanly sportsmanship.

At least for a time – and it was a long time – Lord Hawke and his successors held the upper hand. Professionals could rise to the rank of 'senior professional' – but no higher. It was not until the early 1950s that real cracks started to appear and not until the 1960s (and the disappearance of amateurism) that the structure collapsed. As a consequence, to those of us who started to play first-class cricket at the beginning of the 1950s it was not at all clear what the convention was or indeed whether there still was one at all.

The captaincy of a cricket team is unlike captaincy in other sports. He (or she, as the case may be) is not just there to rally his/her troops on the field of engagement. At all levels of the game, the captain is in addition responsible for tactics – decisions to be made about change of bowlers, field place settings, team morale when things are going wrong, the batting order, and deciding whether and/or when to declare his team's innings closed. In the English county game of the 1950s the burdens were even more extensive. The captain was ultimately responsible for team selection, for making sure his players were paid (and, not least, for negotiating with his amateurs on a proper amount for their expenses), for ensuring that his team all turned up to play on the appointed day – not always easy – and that they were reasonably sober. When travelling, he was responsible for the travel arrangements

– who would go with whom in which car or whether the coach would appear on time or which trains had irrevocably broken down. All in all, he was not just a captain on the field, burdensome as that was, but a paterfamilias to his whole team. By way of assistance, there was little to hand.

There would be a scorer, possibly a physiotherapist and, if the county club was well off, a lad to handle the bags and make sure they arrived at the right destination and in time (less well-off clubs relied on junior professionals to take on this task).

In fact, there was only one helper of importance to hand. It was the senior professional. The 'senior professional' has, as a function, of course now disappeared. It makes no sense to label somebody as 'senior professional' when the captain himself is a professional. To some extent the role has survived informally – a captain nowadays may wish to consult the most experienced member of his side on tactics, field placing and so on. But in the days of the amateur captain the senior professional was much more than a part-time, and frequently perfunctory, adviser. He was a cross between a warrant officer and a trade union official. The system, of course, conformed neatly to the traditional army model in which the young (amateur) lieutenant relied on his experienced and wizened (professional) sergeant major to keep him and the troops steady under fire. (Many films have testified to the strength of the model.)

In practice, the senior professional was often called on for other duties. For instance, the Essex senior professional of the 1950s, Ken Preston, was a natural choice for the secretaryship of the club's Supporters' Association and from there for the management of the club's football pool. This did not, however, detract from his main task (apart from playing cricket) of the players' representative to the captain and the club's committee when they felt that they had a grievance. Nor was his other task overlooked – admonishing from time to time young professionals who had misbehaved.

The final duty was to captain the side when the captain himself was absent, perhaps ill or on Test duty, and where there was no officially appointed vice-captain. In fact, this had regularly been the case before the Second World War. But only one had been appointed for a full season. Ewart Astill, a professional who had been commissioned into the Machine Gun Corps in the First World War, had captained Leicestershire in 1935 since no amateur (although four were approached) wanted the job. He was, as it turned out, rather good at it – Leicestershire came sixth in the county championship in his year – but he was always referred to in committee minutes as 'Astill' and was unceremoniously sacked when the club found a suitable amateur, C. S. Dempster ('Mr Dempster', of course), to take over. Astill, surprisingly good-tempered in such humiliation, was presented by the club with a gold cigarette case for his pains.

After the Second World War reform was very much in the air. In early 1948, Warwickshire appointed H. E. (Tom) Dollery to the joint captaincy with a Cambridge undergraduate, Ron Maudsley. Dollery was to captain the side until Maudsley was available after the University match. The side did well in the early games and Maudsley offered to stand down, but the club committee would have none of it and Maudsley took over. The side then did substantially worse, to the point where the committee, with some hesitation, decided to appoint Dollery for the full season of 1949. Rather to everyone's surprise, Dollery led the side to victory in the county championship of 1951. 1952 was much less successful and Dollery, the hero of 1951, was subject to some unpleasant criticism at the club's annual general meeting. Dollery did not get a gold cigarette case – or anything else.

Dollery's appointment was not immediately followed by others. But it did allow the MCC to consider whether or not the time was ripe for a professional to take charge of the national side. The selectors appointed for this deliberation were R. E. S. ('Bob') Wyatt as Chairman, F. R. ('Freddie') Brown and N. W. D. Yardley, the current captain of Yorkshire. All of them had extensive experience of Test cricket, as had the selector they co-opted, the Kent wicketkeeper Les Ames (as it happened, the first post-war professional to be appointed an England selector). There was plenty of experience in international captaincy as well. Wyatt had captained England as early as 1930, then had been Jardine's vice-captain on the 'bodyline' Ashes tour of 1932–3 (initially a supporter of 'bodyline' tactics but later in the tour with doubts about its morality). He had even captained Worcestershire, at the age of forty-eight, in 1950. Brown, too, had been with Jardine on the 1932–3 tour, and had been drafted in to captain the Ashes tour of 1950–51 (apparently on the basis of hitting a six in the Gentleman vs Players match of 1950 into the window of the pavilion at Lord's where the selectors where sitting at the time). Yardley was also a former England captain, standing in for Hammond in the last Test of the 1946–7 Ashes tour and, not least, captain for the full 1948 series against Australia.

All three of them were amateurs of what used to be described as 'the old school'. Educated privately, Wyatt began his first-class cricket career for Warwickshire in 1923. Dour, rather humourless and with a face like a bull-dog, but affable enough to meet (if slightly pompous), he made his way up the ladder to the England captaincy and from there subsequently to high positions in the MCC. During his playing career he suffered a number of acci-dents at the hands of fast bowlers, the most serious of which occurred when the West Indian Manny Martindale broke his jaw in four places (it is said that when he recov-ered consciousness his first act was to send for a pencil and rearrange the batting order).

Brown was a different kind of fish. He was born in 1910 in Chile and educated there before his parents returned to Britain at the end of the First World War, when he was sent to school and then university at Cambridge. He managed to escape the controversy surrounding the Jardine Ashes tour and went on to play for Surrey until he was commissioned into the Royal Army Service Corps in 1939. Captured at Tobruk in 1942, he spent the rest of the war in a German prisoner-of-war camp. After an unsatisfactory attempt to make a career in the coal indus-try he was sacked in 1949, but was immediately recruited by British Timken as captain and Assistant Secretary of

Northamptonshire, and from there was selected for the Ashes tour of 1950–51.

Brown, as a character, was rumbustious and, when exercised, given to much shouting. Physically, too, he was large – at just over six foot and somewhere around fifteen stone – a self-confident redhead with a jovial manner (at least towards other amateurs) and a habit – which he may have picked up from Jardine – of wearing a white kerchief round his neck when playing and, when not playing, of keeping a pipe firmly stuck in his mouth. But towards professionals he was a martinet. Even after the war they were always addressed by their surnames, instructed to call other amateurs 'Mr so-and-so', never to use the bath in the Northampton pavilion (strictly reserved for himself but occasionally loaned out to visiting – amateur – captains), never to use the showers if there were amateurs who wished to do so and, once the amateurs had finished, to do so in order of seniority. It was, he would say, the way they had done it in the war.

Yardley was from a Yorkshire business family. From Barnsley, where he was born in 1915, he was sent to St Peter's School in York and from there to St John's College, Cambridge. He had already made his name as a young cricketer in Yorkshire but Cambridge proved to be an ideal platform for him. In his first year, 1935, he won his Blue in cricket, squash, hockey and Rugby fives. By 1939 he was thought of as not just a county cricketer but a Test cricketer – and a possible captain both of Yorkshire and England. The war, as with others, intervened and, as an officer in the Green Howards, Yardley served in India and the Middle East before being wounded in Italy in 1944. By 1946 he was ready to return to cricket, was Hammond's vice-captain in the Ashes tour of 1946–7, took over the captaincy of England on Hammond's resignation and of Yorkshire at the start of the 1948 season. He was perhaps unfortunate to have led England against Bradman's Australians in 1948 but, whatever the result, nobody accused Yardley of being unfit for the job.

When Bradman came out to bat in what was to be his last Test innings, at the Oval at the end of the 1948 season, Yardley summoned his team to give his opponent 'three cheers' on his arrival at the wicket. It was a generous gesture, but there were those who thought that he showed too much of the 'amateur spirit' against an opponent who showed none of it at all. The allegation was probably true – there was little evidence there of the will to win. But there was certainly evidence of the much cited 'spirit of the game'. Yardley also treated the Yorkshire professionals, difficult as some of them were, as human beings. He even – unusually for the time – called them by their first names (although they were not allowed to repay the compliment as he insisted on them calling him 'skipper').

The last of the quartet, Les Ames, was also of the 'old school' – but of a different school. Born in Kent, educated in Kent and playing only for Kent (and England), he was a professional in the true sense of the word – regarding cricket as a livelihood, albeit one by choice, rather than as an occasional pastime. He, too, was a veteran of Jardine's Ashes tour of 1932–3, had served in the RAF during the war, had refused to turn amateur to take, when it was offered, the Kent captaincy in 1951 (partly out of pride in his profession but partly also in the knowledge that his captaincy would only last until the stripling Colin Cowdrey was available to replace him) and, finally, had preferred to continue in the role of senior professional, both for Kent and from time to time for England, and virtually make it his own.

It was this unlikely quartet which was to make one of the most momentous decisions in the history of English cricket. The captaincy of England, following the Hawke doctrine, had up till then been the preserve of the amateur. But Yardley had been badly beaten by the Australians in 1948, George Mann had been a success in South Africa in 1948–9 and against New Zealand in 1949 but was not available for the Ashes tour of 1950–51, Freddie Brown had performed competently on that tour and against South Africa in 1951 but had ruled himself out of the 1951–2 tour of India and Pakistan, and the last on the merry-go-round, Nigel Howard, who led the tour, was quite clearly not up to the standard required, even then, to hold his place in the side on ability alone. The selectors were faced with the prospect of a second-rate amateur to captain England against the Indians in 1952 and, more important, against the Australians in 1953. The alternative was to experiment with a professional. After some hesitancy, and some fear about the consequences, they chose the latter.

There was, of course, grumbling from the traditionalists. But fortunately there was one name to hand with which it was difficult to quarrel – Len Hutton. As it happened, the selectors' approach to Hutton came as a complete surprise. It had never occurred to him that the England captain would be anything other than amateur. In fact, when Wyatt first made the offer he suggested to Hutton that it would help matters if he turned amateur. Whatever the undoubted honour, Hutton replied, he could not agree to the condition. It would, his reply made clear, not be in keeping with his background and upbringing. As his wife subsequently made clear, the Moravian culture had bitten too deep.

There is no doubt that the choice of Hutton to captain England eased the way for counties to follow suit. True, a number of counties – initially a majority – remained wedded to amateur captaincy. But there were some significant shifts. Gloucestershire moved to appoint Jack Crapp in 1953, Lancashire followed by appointing Cyril Washbrook in 1954, Northamptonshire appointed Dennis Brookes in the same year, Somerset gave the job to Maurice Tremlett in 1956, Worcestershire settled first for Reg Perks in 1955 and then for Don Kenyon in 1958, and Leicestershire welcomed another disaffected Yorkshireman in Willie Watson to make him captain in the same year. All were tried and tested professionals.

Yet the going was not altogether easy. Surrey, county champions for long years in the 1950s, were captained throughout by amateurs, first by Stuart Surridge and then by Peter May. Yorkshire persisted with Yardley until 1955, then appointed the amateur Billy Sutcliffe (subsequently forced to stand down after a petition from the players) and followed with Ronnie Burnet – certainly a gentleman by any definition, and at least able to sort out the internecine Yorkshire wars, but not able to hold his place as a batsman. Finally, in 1960 a professional, Vic Wilson, was appointed (Len Hutton, although captain of England, had been twice passed over for the job). Hampshire's captaincy remained resolutely amateur with Desmond Eagar passing the job seamlessly on to Colin Ingleby-Mackenzie. Derbyshire, too, kept the faith: Guy Willatt, the Cambridge Blue, captaining until 1955 until Donald Carr, an Oxford Blue, was ready to take over. Essex, too, pledged allegiance to amateurism in the form of one of its most fervent advocates, the former Cambridge captain Doug Insole, as did Glamorgan with Wilf Wooller, Sussex with David Sheppard and Robin Marlar, Nottinghamshire with Reg Simpson and Middlesex with Bill Edrich and John Warr. There was also some backsliding. Reg Perks only lasted a year at Worcester before being replaced by the amateur Peter Richardson; and in 1958 Dennis Brookes was similarly displaced by the amateur Raman Subba Row who had been head-hunted from Surrey for the purpose; and Warwickshire returned to amateur captaincy in 1957.

Professional captains undoubtedly brought with them a change in the style of leadership. Not for nothing were Washbrook and George Emmett (successor to Jack Crapp at Gloucester) both nicknamed 'Captain Bligh'. Possibly in response, however, though possibly as a reflection of the way the game was developing, there was an equivalent change in the style of amateur leadership. By the mid-1950s amateurs, led by May, had generally become much more determined in their approach to the game. The desire to win had overtaken the desire to have a good time – even

Ingleby-Mackenzie, the last of the amateur captains to treat county cricket as an extension of Old Etonian jollity, led Hampshire to the championship in 1961 (although he led a group of very concentrated professionals). Surridge was a good example of the new breed. Not only was he fierce with the egos of his main bowlers, Bedser, Loader, Laker and Lock, but he was equally aggressive towards opposing batsmen whom he found irritating – in other words if they made too many runs. Wooller was another example. A bruiser of a man (he had played rugby for Wales) he was not interested, as he used to say himself, in playing pat ball. His language to batsmen, particularly when he was bowling himself, was more than usually foul – and he was on occasion, not to put too fine a point on it, reckless in bending the rules of the game to suit his purpose. Marlar was an equally robust captain and even the otherwise mild-mannered Reg Simpson could be gratuitously sarcastic on the field. (In fact, Wooller, Marlar and Simpson were hardly on speaking terms for a number of years.)

The truth is that the amateur captains were becoming more like their professional brothers. This was not confined to their approach to the game. By the mid-1950s it had become clear to all but the most blinkered county club committees that the game had moved beyond the days when an amateur could simply saunter in or out of the side as and when it suited his convenience. Amateurs in general had to show that they deserved their place in the side. But it was doubly true of captains. It was no longer enough to wait for the end of a university or a school term to pull in an amateur to replace whoever was in charge up till then. Amateur captains, like professional captains who took the job as part of their employment, had – barring Test match duties – to take charge full time for a whole season.

The problem was that nobody could meet that commitment as a pure, unsullied amateur. They either had to have, or to have married, substantial fortunes (e.g. Cowdrey, Ingleby-Mackenzie, Surridge) or to have employers who deliberately employed them on a basis that allowed them as much time as they needed for cricket (e.g. May, Warr, Insole, Brown, Subba Row, Simpson, Marlar – the last an unlikely archivist for the Duke of Norfolk at Arundel Castle) or to have been allocated jobs within the county club of their affiliation such as Secretary or Assistant Secretary (e.g. Wooller, Bailey, Smith, Richardson, Eagar, Carr).

In practice, it was this last category that most irritated the professionals, since the beneficiaries were in truth professionals in all but name. Yet there was nothing illegal in the arrangements. If a private members' club such as a county cricket club wished to employ people, and allow them time off for an activity which was only marginally related to their employment, it was all one to them. Certainly, the MCC, another members' club which employed secretaries and assistant secretaries, could hardly object. But the professionals had a point, as Frank Tyson, for one, kept on repeating.

By 1957 the nature of captaincy had changed from the cavalier Corinthian days of popular mythology. The 'amateur' captains' fearful trip – and at times, as in Australia in 1932–3, it was fearful – was done. Professionalism, in its many aspects and in all its meanings, was taking over. In fact, it was taking over as fast as the game itself was changing.

5

THE GAME

Play up! Play up! and play the game!

Cricket has never been simple. For a start, nobody knows with any certainty where it came from or how or when it began. Some cricket historians assert with confidence that the game is of Flemish origin; others are sure that a version of the game was played in the early 1300s by a son of King Edward I; more claim that it can be traced accurately to around 1550 when it was played at a school in Guildford. On surer ground, there are references to it in the early seventeenth-century courts – in 1624 a player was apparently killed by a ball landing on his head. Together with other games it was later on put by the Puritans in the same category as dancing and the theatre, and consequently prohibited, as a threat to the salvation of the immortal soul. It was only with the Restoration in 1660 that the game (again, like dancing and the theatre) was legalised as a popular entertainment, along with the previous habit of gambling on the result. Thus relaunched, it never looked back – at least, for a few centuries until football took over as the English national game.

It would, of course, be a mistake to imagine that 'creck-ett', as it was then known (the spelling was variable) bore much relation to the game we knew in the 1950s or to the game as it is now. The bowling was underarm, the ball being rolled along the ground towards a single wicket. To meet this rather sneaky delivery the batsman had a bat which looked much like a modern hockey stick – a straight shaft with a curved end. From those ill-defined beginnings, the first major change took place when bowl-ers started to pitch the ball rather than rolling it along the ground. To deal with that, even though the ball was still bowled underarm, the bat had to be redesigned to become straight and flat like the bat of today. The next major change was the admission of round-arm and then over-arm bowling in the middle and late nineteenth century. Both of them led to consequential changes in the bats-man's stance and to the adoption of leg pads to protect the shins and gloves to protect the hands.

By the end of the nineteenth century the game had come at least to resemble the game which I was brought up to play in my childhood before and during the Second World War. In fact, between 1900 and 1950 there were only three changes of consequence in what should prop-erly be called the 'Laws' of cricket. These laws were determined, odd as it may now seem, by the MCC, the exclusive members' club as it was – and still is (strangely, the MCC to this day still holds the copyright of the Laws although it has no responsibility for making them). Of the three changes, two were relatively insignificant. In 1927, the cricket ball was made slightly smaller to allow a better grip and hence more purchase and thus more turn for spinners. In 1931 the stumps – by then there were three – were made an inch higher and wider. The third, and by far the most significant change, which affected the whole conduct of the game, was in the 1935 leg before wicket (lbw) law.

Until 1934 a batsman could only be given out lbw if the ball pitched in line between wicket and wicket, hit part of his body (apart from the gloves which were considered to be part of his bat) and would, in the opinion of the umpire, have gone on to hit his wicket. This law undoubtedly favoured the batsman. He could kick any ball away which pitched either to the off or to the leg of the line between wicket and wicket. Both Jack Hobbs, always said to be the most elegant of batsmen, and Herbert Sutcliffe, the Yorkshire opening bat in the interwar years, were masters of the technique. With flat and lifeless pitches also helping the batsman, large scores were piled up. In the 1920s timeless matches were tried but the only result was that even larger scores were made. In Australia, for instance, in two timeless games 1,000 runs were made in one innings and in the 1934 English season fourteen batsmen averaged more than fifty in first-class cricket. By then it had become apparent that change was needed if the balance between bat and ball was to be fairer. Later in the year the MCC adopted a new law, to come into force in 1935, that a batsman could be out even if the ball had pitched outside the off stump – provided always that it hit him in line.

The new law generated much heated discussion. In fact, the debate rumbled on into the 1950s. There were those who maintained that bowlers were now encouraged to concentrate on inswing and off spin, which was seen to be negative (although quite why it should be was never plausibly explained). Certainly leg spin bowling was put at a comparative disadvantage, since the blanket rule that a batsman could not be given out lbw if the ball had pitched outside leg stump was maintained. Bradman, in the late 1930s, thought that the law should be extended to include contact with the batsman outside the off stump. Hutton advocated the adoption of four stumps. Washbrook wanted a reversion to the pre-1935 law. Almost all senior professionals, in a review carried out in 1956, thought that the 1935 law was, one way or another, a dreadful mistake.

In practice, the change had at least some of its intended effect. Batsmen became much less prolific. In 1935 no batsman averaged over fifty in first-class cricket. Nevertheless, as time went by counter-measures were devised. By the early 1950s batsmen had developed a more sophisticated technique to combat the ball coming into the bat from the off. Because of the reluctance of umpires to give lbw decisions in the bowler's favour if the ball hit the batsman's front leg, and because the law still insisted that the ball must hit the batsman between wicket and wicket, it was possible to push the front pad outside that line and allow the ball coming in from the off to hit it – while not offering a stroke. Both May and Cowdrey were adept at this (but it did not take long for the rest of us to learn). The result was some very boring cricket when the weather was benign and the pitch was flat.

The cricket was much less boring when there was rain about or when the pitch was anything but flat. Throughout the 1950s the only parts of the ground which could be covered during a match were the small sections (not more than three feet six inches beyond the popping crease, the law made clear) where the bowler put his feet down in his last stride. The reason for this exemption was obvious. The bowler risked serious damage to his ankles or knees if he slipped on wet turf. The clear intention, however, was to leave the playing surface open to rain or sun, or whatever else nature provided.

The result was that both batsmen and bowlers had to acquire skills (and captains had to learn tactics) which were different to those of the modern game. Batsmen had to adapt to a wholly changed pitch if, for instance, they had started their innings on a fine day and a benign pitch only to find that they were to continue it on the following day on a rain-affected wicket with the ball spitting and turning. Moreover, it was not just a question of rain. Heavy dew could leave a pitch on the opening day of a match green to the point where a good seam bowler, such as a Bedser or a Bailey, could move the ball off the seam at speed and require instant adjustment. If he had weathered that particular storm, the batsman might find, after an hour or so, that he was batting on a benign, if fast, pitch. At that point, if he had settled in, he might have to face the flight of a leg spinner trying to induce him into a false stroke. (The last thing he would have faced was a left-arm finger spinner bowling over the wicket with depressing negativity into the bowler's footmarks at the opposite end.)

The skills which bowlers had to acquire were no less daunting. Seam bowlers, fast or medium-paced, had to learn how to exploit not just the new ball with its classic swing but all the variations of a wicket which might be wet, green, drying out or dusty. Finger spin bowlers had to learn how to flight the delivery on dry wickets and increase the pace and bite when on a wet or drying wicket. Wrist spinners had to calculate how to lure batsmen into error by flight alone or by a faster spin (and by disguising its final direction) and then wait to take advantage of a crumbling wicket on the third day.

Furthermore, because of the peripatetic nature of much county cricket in the 1950s, both batsmen and bowlers had to understand, and adjust to, the vagaries of the club grounds on which they played. It was useful to know, for instance, that at Hove or Westcliff the pitch became noticeably greener as the tide came in with a moist onshore breeze, or that the wicket at Brentwood had a definite hole in the middle, or that Pontypridd had a short mid-wicket boundary, or that Bristol resembled a sandpit. Knowledge of such local conditions could be of vital importance. It was also useful to know whom the opponents had selected for a particular match. It was widely suspected, for instance, that the Essex wickets were deliberately left with plentiful grass on them when Bailey was available to bowl.

Quite apart from the techniques required by bat and ball to flourish in such conditions (most of which seem to have disappeared from the modern game), selectors were presented with their own problems. If there was rain about it was vital to play one or even two finger spinners who could take advantage of a rain-affected wicket. If there had been overnight dew it was important to play quick bowlers who could move the ball off the seam. If there was cloud, swing bowlers could profit. If it was dry and dusty, wrist spinners came into their own. The selection of batsmen also could be difficult. The amateurs who had learnt their trade at public school and played mostly on the front foot could find themselves in difficulty against a well-directed seam attack on a green wicket. The professionals, on the other hand, generally more cautious and on the back foot, were apt to allow spinners to pin them down.

There is also no doubt that county cricket in the 1950s was more sedate than it is today. There was no one-day or limited-over competition. Umpires were treated with friendly respect rather than as objects to be shouted at. Appeals were muted affairs rather than hysterical screams. There were only modest celebrations when a wicket was taken and, above all, there were no worldly wise commentators looking at television replays and deciding that the umpire had made a mistake.

This is not to say that the game was free from controversy. In fact, in one particular, there was a lively debate about what constituted a 'no ball'. It was generally acknowledged that throwing was illegal – but it was often difficult to tell when a bowler was bowling with a straight arm or when his arm was bent. Much more difficult, however, was the decision which the umpire at the bowler's end had to make on whether or not the bowler's trailing foot had been in front of the bowling crease at the point of delivery (known as 'dragging'). It was widely believed, in fact we all assumed without further argument, that Lindwall had been guilty of this in 1948 (Lindwall was a fearsome enough bowler at any time but he was even more difficult to play if he was bowling from twenty yards instead of the statutory twenty-two). In the event, there were various remedies canvassed, the most popular of which was to draw a line a foot or so behind the bowling crease and to tell the bowler not to put his trailing foot down over the line. That was all very well, but it made the umpire's job even more difficult. It was hard enough to look at the bowling crease to see where the bowler's foot had transgressed and then to look up to follow the ball in case there was an appeal for lbw or a catch at the wicket. It was made doubly hard if the umpire had to look at a line behind the bowling crease as well. In truth, even with the present front-foot no-ball law, it would be foolhardy to say that the matter has been fully resolved.

Apart from developments in the laws of cricket in the 1950s, there were other changes. Of course, the equipment that we carried on our travels and the clothes that we wore were heavier than those of today – apart from the bats which were lighter (typically, we would use a bat of 2.8lb (1.28kg) while today's bats are 3.0lb (1.36kg) and sometimes more). Our shirts were of flannel, our trousers of heavy cotton, our socks and sweaters of wool and our boots of light leather or heavy canvas with leather soles and metal studs. Our equipment, too, was less elaborate, if heavier, than today's. For obvious reasons the design of the protector – of a batsman's most sensitive parts – has not changed but leg pads were more primitive and gloves little more than cotton gloves with a protective layer of rubber above the fingers. Thigh pads, chest pads and helmets were unknown (although sometimes we stuffed towels into our trousers for protection) – in fact, many batsmen, Compton, May, Insole and Bailey being prime examples, preferred to bat bare-headed without even a cap.

Nevertheless, more than the peripheral changes in the laws or the primitive nature of the equipment, it was the nature of the audience which changed the game irreversibly in the 1950s. Cricket was the one sport which could be followed by all classes and, in the period immediately after the Second World War, when there was food rationing, clothes rationing, prohibitions of every sort, it met the desire for something joyful and splendid. Even the humiliation of England by the Australians in 1948 was accepted, rather as the unfortunate result of a contest between brothers. In those days, it was possible to hear a discussion of cricket in most pubs and even the Prime Minister of the day, Clement Attlee, called for the cricket scores of the previous day before all else.

The change started unexpectedly. In 1950 at the Oval we suddenly heard the calypso, 'those little pals of mine, Ramadhin and Valentine'. In the bank below the gasometer was a crowd of Caribbean faces. They were singing, of course, for the West Indian tourists who, for the first time (although even then they were captained by the white John Goddard), were proving equal to their former colonial masters. There was much official disapproval of the demonstration – alcohol was believed (incorrectly) to have provoked it – but one thing was immediately clear. They were here, in south London, and they meant to stay. What Winston Churchill was to call the 'magpie society' was already with us.

Throughout the 1950s there was much debate as to whether there should or should not be controls on immigration, but it was difficult to frame legislation which would allow citizens of the 'white' Commonwealth free access to the United Kingdom and ration access from the 'coloured' Commonwealth. The result was that the flow of Caribbean immigration continued and was soon augmented by migrants from Asia, particularly the Indian sub-continent. In net figures, to be sure, the balance for the UK was negative in that more British whites emigrated between 1946 and 1950 than Commonwealth coloured arrived. But there was no doubt that attendances at cricket matches started to reflect the arrival of Caribbean and Indian (and Pakistani) immigrants. Although cricket was said to be a unifying factor – it had, after all, been the premier game of the British Empire – there was in this new and unfamiliar world, with different loyalties, some anti-colonial emotion from the immigrants and some blatantly racist attitudes from their new British neighbours. What was beyond doubt, however, was that none of the new cricket onlookers had any understanding of, and therefore any sympathy for, the distinction between amateur and professional.

The same, in fact, was true of migrants from the 'white' Commonwealth. Australians, Canadians, New Zealanders and South Africans who came to Britain after the Second World War, Australians in particular, coming as they did from a more egalitarian society, thought the distinction a bad joke. When Lindsay Hassett, captain of Australia in their Ashes tour of 1953, was invited to share the amateurs' dressing room at the Oval with the Surrey amateurs he burst out laughing (a rare event for him) and replied that he would be torn limb from limb by his players if he accepted the invitation. Australian spectators, too, were less restrained than their English counterparts and, with all the handed-down memories of the Jardine tour of 1932–3, singled out amateurs both at the Oval and Lords for some characteristic abuse.

Others from the 'white' Commonwealth were not so vocal. But the sentiments were the same. What they all shared, however, was physical health. Not to put too fine a point on it, they were, in comparison to their British brothers and sisters, better clothed and better fed. For a start, clothes in Britain had only come off rationing in 1948, but even then the government persisted with its guidelines for manufacturers until 1952. The colours were still those of wartime – grey, brown and black. That was not at all what Canadians, Australians and New Zealanders were wearing. Clothing had never been rationed in their countries and bright colours in summer for sporting events were the unchallenged fashion. Gradually, the fashion for sporting – and leisure generally – dress spread to Britain. For women it was the age of ready-to-wear, relatively cheap, brightly coloured blouses and skirts (and even, for the very daring, trousers) and for men the suits issued on demobilisation, badly cut and universally in grey or navy blue, gave way to slacks and T-shirts. Seen by at least one observer from the wicket the crowds which at the beginning of the decade seemed no more than a sea of grey (in the northern towns with a topping of flat caps) started to look in the mid- and late 1950s kaleidoscopically coloured.

They also looked, at least to me, somewhat plumper. Although the wartime diet had been for many working-class families an improvement on the near starvation of the 1930s, rationing had been hard on the middle class (those higher up the social ladder had their own barely concealed ways of supplementing their rations). Basic foods, such as meat, butter, cheese, sugar, bacon and cooking fat, were on ration from 1940 or 1941 until late 1953 or the spring of 1954. Even bread had been rationed from July 1946 to July 1948 and tea from 1940 to 1952 and sweets from 1942 to 1953.

The lifting of food rationing led, like the lifting of clothes rationing, to a revolution in both quantity and taste. Between 1950 and 1960 the consumption of sugar (per person per week) rose 70 per cent, of beef and veal 10 per cent, of fresh green vegetables 15 per cent and of fresh fruit 40 per cent. In decline were the staple foods of wartime. Potatoes went down 6 per cent and sausages (such as they were) 10 per cent. It was, of course, a healthy change. It was only later on that it was noted that the consumption of fats and sweets had risen almost exponentially and would bring their own health problems.

It was not just a question of quantities. After May 1954, when rationing finally ended, we could eat as much as we wanted (or could pay for) wherever we wanted. Italian restaurants suddenly became the vogue. Cookery books were published with instructions on how to select basic ingredients and cook them well but also with exotic recipes from countries never hitherto heard of as producers of wonderful dishes. Foreign travel brought not just food but wines to the British taste. Where before in any cricket pavilion only beer had been served as the decade went on there was a choice of wines.

Furthermore, in the peace of the early 1950s, there were holidays to be enjoyed – Butlins was a great and popular feature at Clacton-on-Sea where we cricketers were entertained, with a generous but, if the truth were known, a somewhat overwhelming enthusiasm. Blackpool, Scarborough and Southend, to take only three examples, were able to combine their traditional festivities with a week of first-class cricket.

And yet, even by the middle of the decade, there had come a marked change. Television had finally arrived. Until 1953 television had been a medium reserved for a small minority of affluent viewers. The take-up of licences had been small. In 1948 only 45,000 TV licences had been issued (as against over eleven million for radio). The figure had crept up to over 300,000 by 1952. But what caused an explosion in the numbers was the Coronation of 1953.

It so happened that it was only after official and ministerial wrangling – and an ultimate decision by the Prime Minister Winston Churchill himself – that it was finally agreed that the service should be broadcast from inside Westminster Abbey – to the accompaniment of a sonorous commentary from Richard Dimbleby. The BBC hastily scrabbled to make the necessary arrangements. Almost immediately, over half a million television sets were sold in the build-up to the ceremony and, although the total of sets only rose to 2.3 million, when the day came some twenty million people – 40 per cent of the population – crowded around them to watch. The sale of licences thereafter grew rapidly, reaching just over 10 million in 1960.

Once they had bought their sets and their licences, viewers had a problem. To say the least, it could not be said that the programmes offered at the time by the BBC were particularly entertaining. They were, of course, in black and white (colour transmissions did not make even a hesitant start until 1967). There were also externally imposed restrictions. It was not until July 1957, for instance, that the Fourteen Day Rule, which prevented the BBC from discussing on any medium issues which Parliament would be debating during the following fortnight, was lifted by Prime Minister Harold Macmillan, and there was no news on television at all until 1954. In 1954, however, the passage of the Television Act allowed commercial television to compete openly with the BBC. Starting in September 1955 in the south of England, Independent Television became available in the Midlands in January 1956, Lancashire in May 1956, Yorkshire in November 1956, Scotland in August 1957, Wales and the South West in August 1958. By then the proportion of the population within the range of both BBC and ITV had reached 80 per cent.

The arrival of ITV certainly galvanised the BBC. Yet both channels were slow to recognise the possibilities of televising sport. The first *Sportsview*, on 8 April 1954, contained no more than a commentary on a motor cycle speedway event. The viewing figures were unimpressive. In the summer of 1955 the programme moved from Thursday to Wednesday night and immediately became more popular. But there were two difficulties. The first was that both BBC and ITV considered sport to be part of 'outside broadcasts'. They therefore had to compete for attention with royal events, natural disasters, serious accidents and so on. Secondly, the sports authorities were in no mood to allow television to steal their audiences and either refused permission to broadcast or imposed such restrictions as to make broadcasting at best uneconomic and at worst futile. Needless to say, it took time for these difficulties to be addressed, let alone overcome.

It was not until October 1958 that *Grandstand* went on air on Saturday afternoons. After a shaky start it made a profound impact. Although many sports were still embargoed (cricket and football leading the field), there was enough sport on a Saturday afternoon to engage the attention of all but the most dedicated football or cricket fanatic. Gradually, Saturday afternoons came for many to be sessions in front of a television set instead of a visit to the ground. In fact, once divorced from his or her habitual afternoon at the ground, it was not hard to find other recreations which became available in the prosperity of the 1950s.

In all this, it comes as no surprise to find that attendances at county and Test cricket matches started to dwindle. The post-war spike in enthusiasm – in 1947, 2.3 million people paid to watch first-class cricket – had already declined by 1950. The decline went faster in the 1950s with the arrival of television so that by 1960 the figure was only just over one million, or a daily average on all grounds of below 1,500. The financial consequences were, for the county clubs, little short of disastrous. As private members' clubs they were in difficulties already. In fact, their predicament could only get worse. Indeed, it came to the point where some of them in the late 1950s could hardly afford to pay their players – which, oddly enough, made the amateurs (on expenses) all the more valuable as substitutes to salaried professionals. The conclusion was obvious. It was time for the clubs to look seriously at what really mattered: the money.

6

WHAT ABOUT THE MONEY?

*'No gentleman ought to make a profit by his
services in the cricket field'*

No sooner had Jim Laker been selected for the Ashes tour of Australia in 1958–9 than he asked to see Gubby Allen, the then Chairman of the board of selectors, on an urgent matter. The interview was, naturally enough, granted on request. But Allen, as it turned out, was in for a surprise. In the interview, Laker asked whether it would be possible for him to opt to go as an amateur rather than as a professional. Allen, visibly taken aback, had to think for a few moments before giving his reply.

After a pause Allen then played, as it were, for time. He asked Laker – in his best patriarchal manner – whether he had fully considered the advantages and disadvantages of turning amateur at what was, after all, a late stage in his cricket career. Laker replied that indeed he had, but that he thought he would be better off financially if he could be an amateur at least – and only – for the tour and return to his professional career thereafter. He said that Trevor Bailey had told him that, as an amateur, he was to receive for the tour £1,000 in allowance for expenses (tax-free – and in addition to his salary from Essex) while he, Laker, as a professional, was only to be paid a taxable £800. If he could tour as an amateur he would get the same reward as Bailey – and could then return as a professional for Surrey the following season. It all seemed perfectly logical, although Laker's figures about Bailey's allowance are improbable, to say the least, and Bailey may have been having a quiet joke at the rather solemn Laker's expense. But in the event Allen, as Laker related it, 'was not best pleased', and the request was abruptly refused.

Laker, of course, was serious about wishing to have the rate for the job, whether it was done by an amateur or a professional. But he was also making a point – in his usual blunt fashion. The point was simple: amateurs were being paid more than professionals for doing the same job. To add fuel to the flame, it was only a few months later that Laker discovered, much to his further irritation, that the amateur Peter May (his county captain) had won £500 from an Australian newspaper for scoring a century between lunch and tea and had, in the same week, formed a limited company to protect his overall receipts from any unwelcome attention from the UK Inland Revenue.

In fact, Laker's point was well made. He, of course, like Tyson and Trueman, had been a serial complainer about 'shamateurism', and by the end of the 1950s they seemed to have even greater reason. Yet it was not a new problem, and Laker should not, if he had studied the history (which he had not), have been unduly surprised.

Amateurs in the past had notoriously claimed 'expenses' which were well in excess of their disbursements and

had been accordingly paid – tax-free. (The most fla-
grant example had been Gilbert Jessop, the flamboyant
Gloucestershire batsman renowned for hitting a ball over
the old pavilion at Lord's, in the 'golden age' before the
First World War.) By contrast, professionals not only
had to pay most of their own expenses but had relied on
their salaries to keep house and home. This divide had no
doubt been tolerable for a time for what was, after all, a
master/servant relationship, but over the years, at least in
the latter part of the nineteenth century, the professional
grumbling had started to become perceptibly louder in
volume.

As it happened, in the second half of the nineteenth
century there was a clear target for professional com-
plaint. The chief culprits were no less than the Grace
brothers, W. G. and E. M. The brothers' joint efforts in
exploiting the system to maximise financial reward while
maintaining amateur status were both remarkably imaginative and relentlessly effective. During the 1870s W. G.
Grace earned, if that is the right word, in every season
something close to £40,000 in today's values. He did this
by a number of devices. When asked to promote matches,
for instance of a United South Eleven in Scotland in
1872, he required an upfront fee of £100 (some £4,500
today). The professionals were to be paid £5 (£300) and
the profit would naturally accrue to himself. He would
also then claim attendance fees, judging (correctly) that
he would be the main attraction for the crowds. In 1878,
again, his brother E. M. submitted an invoice to Surrey
County Cricket Club for a match with Gloucestershire at
the Oval – which Surrey themselves were expected to pay.

Fifteen pounds was claimed for W. G. (£700 today). Nor did E. M. neglect his own interests: £20 attendance fee (just under £1,000 today) for the match. Then, of course, there were expenses.

The domestic matches were a steady source of income for the 'amateur' Grace brothers, but the really big money for W. G. started to come from MCC tours to Australia. In 1873, he was invited to tour Australia. It could not be done, he claimed, without a fee of £1,500 (some £70,000 today) plus expenses for himself and his family. In 1891 he was again invited to tour Australia. By that time his fee had doubled to £3,000 (now worth some £180,000) plus the usual expenses. The professionals recruited for the same tour remarked caustically that they were paid a taxable £300 plus expenses.

Even in those relatively carefree days the financial ambitions of the Grace brothers raised a storm. In November 1878 the MCC Committee met to consider the whole matter. The result of their deliberations was a statement that 'no gentleman ought to make a profit by his services in the cricket field, and that for the future no cricketer who takes more than his expenses in any match shall be qualified to play for the Gentlemen against the Players at Lord's'. The statement was immediately, and rightly, derided.

It went from bad to worse when the MCC claimed that this had been the existing position which in the past had been meticulously observed. This was, of course, patently untrue. Yet the statement showed a surprising degree of subtlety. By specifying 'services in the cricket field' the MCC was able conveniently to ignore payments to amateurs either before they arrived at the 'cricket field' or after they had left the 'cricket field' or services outside the 'cricket field'. As such, the voracious financial appetite of the Grace brothers could easily be excused. After all, W. G. (and to a lesser extent E. M.) drew the crowds in and the editor of *Wisden* in the end was, in the edition of 1897, able to write, without apparent shame or irony, that 'Mr W. G. Grace's position has for years, as everyone knows, been an anomalous one, but "nice customs curtsey to great kings"'.

But this was not enough for the 'great king'. W. G. had one final requirement: a National Testimonial Fund in his honour. This was launched in 1895 with a trumpet fanfare of press publicity. Such was the enthusiasm that, in all, the Fund raised just over £9,000 (just over £500,000 today). Apart from all else, it allowed Grace a comfortable retirement when he chose to take it. Indeed, in the course of time and with the proceeds in his pocket he duly retired – as an amateur.

Although the amount raised in Grace's testimonial was by the standards of the day exceptional, the principle of testimonials for long-serving amateurs was, at least until the First World War, generally accepted. ('Testimonials' were for amateurs; professionals received 'benefits' – a none too subtle distinction.) So, too, was the habit of county clubs giving presents to notable amateurs on their weddings, on retirement or simply if they felt like it. In 1904, for instance, Sussex members clubbed together to give their star batsman C. B. Fry a motor car – for no apparent reason but pronounced to be in recognition of his performances for the county. (Cricket was not his only distinction. He was also an Olympic athlete and had been offered the throne of Albania.) Gilbert Jessop was not in the least deterred from claiming whatever could be extracted from his county club, Gloucestershire. The Grace brothers, from the same county had, after all, paved the way.

None of this was much encouragement to professionals, obliged, as they were, to live on their wages. By the end of the nineteenth century, many of them had belatedly started to recognise their financial position – and, indeed, their social position – simply as 'hired labourers of the game'. That said, they were not left entirely destitute, at least while they were playing. In 1900, for instance, a senior professional could earn, from salary and a variety of bonuses, between £16,500 and £20,000 in today's values. True, it was far from generous but it was at least above the average wage of a skilled worker at the time. In addition, a prominent long-serving player could expect to be awarded a benefit – at the discretion, of course, of his employing county club. The usual formula was for the player to receive the proceeds of one match, together with any other revenues which might come with it. (In fact, it took many years and a decision of the House of Lords to determine that the proceeds of benefits were not subject to income tax.)

In the years between the two World Wars the picture was far from the pre-First World War 'golden age'. It was one of mass unemployment in which most professional cricketers felt that they were lucky to have a job at all. By 1932, for instance, unemployment had risen to 23 per cent generally and to 41 per cent in the coal mining industry

Afternoon break in the Ashes Test at Leeds in July 1938; Bradman sitting in the foreground

A leg glance: author in Oxford vs Cambridge, 1954

Summer in the Oxford Parks

Peter May: August 1952

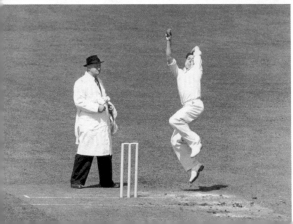

(*above*) Ted Dexter:
September 1961

(*middle left*) Colin Cowdrey:
June 1967

(*bottom left*) Trevor Bailey:
May 1950

David Sheppard:
street cricket in 1956

All together in the
Second World War:
back row (far right)
Sgt Len Hutton;
(third from right)
Major G.O. Allen;
front row (second
from right)
Lt F.R. Brown

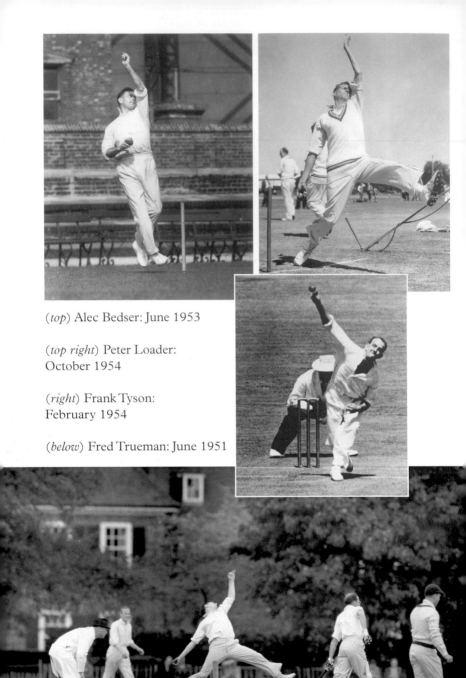

(*top*) Alec Bedser: June 1953

(*top right*) Peter Loader: October 1954

(*right*) Frank Tyson: February 1954

(*below*) Fred Trueman: June 1951

Len Hutton
stacking
shelves in his
Bradford shop:
January 1953

Cyril
Washbrook
with some
very attentive
schoolboys:
February 1957

(*left*) Duke Bernard

(*below*) Cover page of
the Duke's 1957 report

REPORT OF THE SPECIAL
COMMITTEE
appointed by the
M.C.C.
to examine
Amateur Status
1957

Chairman : The Duke of Norfolk

Members :

Mr. H. S. Altham	Mr. C. G. Howard
Mr. G. O. Allen	Mr. D. J. Insole
Mr. M. J. C. Allom	Mr. P. B. H. May
Col. R. J. de C. Barber	Mr. C. H. Palmer
Mr. F. R. Brown	Col. R. S. Rait Kerr
Mr' E. D. R. Eagar	Mr. A. B. Sellers
Mr. C. A. F. Hastilow	Rev. D. S. Sheppard

Freddie Brown

Harry Altham

Brian Sellers

Rowan Rait Kerr

Gubby Allen

Doug Insole

W.G. Grace with his money

GOOD OLD GRACE

100 000/-

ALLY SLOPER'S HALF HOLIDAY.
OCT. 5. 1895.

... George Dunnet

"IT MUST BE A GREAT RELIEF FOR THEM NOT TO HAVE TO BE
GENTLEMEN ANY MORE"

from which many professionals were recruited. Under those circumstances the pressure on cricketers' earnings was unremitting. In fact, when the National Government, in the emergency budget of September 1931, cut unemployment benefit by 10 per cent and teachers' salaries by 15 per cent, the county committees were quick to seize their chance and to reduce professional cricketers' wages by an average 10 per cent. By 1939 the seasonal maximum agreed between the counties was down to £440 (approximately £12,600 in today's values). Nor was there much prospect of winter work for those who were not selected for overseas tours. Moreover, county clubs realised that it was always cheaper to play amateurs than to keep professionals on their books. Amateurs could come and go as needed and the professionals could be, and were, dismissed without compensation.

In 1944, towards the end of the Second World War, the counties suggested that the pre-war arrangements should be reinstated without change. Nobody in the Advisory County Cricket Committee of the MCC (ACCC), the body which determined such matters, had seemed to realise that the whole atmosphere of the game – indeed of the social world – had changed with the war. Clubs were advised to reimpose the pre-war financial straitjacket: amateurs would be paid their expenses and professionals would be paid a salary similar to their pre-war rate – in other words, a maximum of £440.

The reason given, in good faith, was the necessity for tightening the collective belt of the immediate post-war years. There were, of course, no luxuries; there was rationing, and none of the things which we easily take for granted today was available – sliced bread, microwaves, dishwashers, let alone motorways. All in all, the cost of fighting a long war had to be borne by everybody, and cricket was part of a society in relative penury.

Nevertheless, the programme of financial restraint was soon to be unworkable. The county club ranks were broken – first by Surrey and then, soon after, by Lancashire. By 1947 a capped Surrey professional was awarded £550 a year (compared with average male earnings in manufacturing of £370 a year), between £13,000 and £14,000 today. In addition there was always the prospect of further income from advertising or sponsorship. At Lancashire a compromise was reached to ensure that all capped players would receive a minimum salary of £416 which, together with match fees, win bonuses and performance bonuses ('talent money'), could bring the total to £600. In addition essential expenses were met – although the pre-war practice of giving allowances for overnight accommodation was abandoned when it was found that many professionals had taken to sleeping rough and simply pocketing the allowance. Other clubs soon fell into line. A junior professional at Essex, for instance, in 1948 could expect to be paid an annual £350 with match fees and win money (when he was selected and if the county won), which, with luck, could make his total remuneration up to the minimum.

Professionals, however, did rather better than amateurs. In the days of post-war austerity amateurs' expenses came under detailed scrutiny. But there was the worry that amateurism could die out altogether. On 1 November 1948 Errol Holmes, the Surrey captain, wrote to the Secretary of the MCC, Colonel Rowan Rait Kerr, to the effect that the experienced amateur would soon die out and the game would become wholly professional. The MCC should do something about this – although Holmes had no specific remedy to offer. Rait Kerr, in his reply, was sympathetic. He acknowledged that 'the red light was burning before 1939 and the subject was broached at the select committee in 1944 but for very good reasons left alone' before going on – rather tartly – to write that 'I am not surprised that you have not suggested any way out of the difficulty'.

The upshot was a letter sent just before Christmas 1948 by Ronald Aird, Assistant Secretary of the MCC, to all county cricket clubs. Rather ominously, the letter started by saying 'it would appear possible that at some future date it may become necessary to examine the whole question of what expenses can be allowed to amateurs without jeopardising their status'. It went on, however, not just to ask counties 'what expenses they regard as justifiable at present' but also to enquire, obviously mindful of the Holmes letter to Rait Kerr, 'in what directions, if any, it is desirable to provide greater latitude'.

Judging from the responses to Aird's letter as they came in over the winter, there was a good deal of huffing and puffing among the retired military officers who peopled the county committees. Some replied as though the whole question was offensive (Leicestershire on 6 January and Essex on 18 January 1949). Others were more forthcoming, stating that third-class rail fares should be allowed (first-class for Yorkshire) or a cash amount in lieu for car travel, hotel accounts without drinks, taxis where necessary and 'gratuities to porters' (Somerset on 10 January,

Gloucestershire on 13 January and Yorkshire on 18 January). But, with two exceptions, there was no appetite for 'greater latitude'.

The exceptions were Glamorgan and Northamptonshire. In his letter to Aird of 31 December J. C. Clay, the Glamorgan club Secretary, put his finger on the problem which had been vexing Errol Holmes and Rait Kerr. 'It is assumed', he wrote, 'that the over-riding object is to get all the best cricketers into first class cricket and that the financial side should therefore be made as easy as possible for all those who for one reason or another cannot become professionals.' Clay went on to write that the whole question of expenses seemed to turn on the matter of 'broken time', in other words salary or wages forfeited by amateurs who were good enough to play first-class cricket and who, on the Holmes/Rait Kerr principle, should be encouraged to do so. Colonel Coldwell, the Northamptonshire Secretary, was even more forthright. In his letter to Aird of 18 January 1949, Coldwell reported his committee as opining that 'greater latitude should be allowed. If an amateur has to lose salary by playing cricket, this should be made up to him as out of pocket expenses. If we are to retain and encourage amateurs for county cricket, there should be no quibble at this at all.'

A less choleric – and more studied – view was taken by Surrey County Cricket Club. In due fashion they set up their own sub-committee to consider the matter. The expenses met by the club, the sub-committee reported, should be for fares, hotels and drinks at meals and hotel tips, meals and drinks on the train and necessary taxis and tips. So far, as it were, so good. But the sub-committee went on to recommend that amateurs should be reimbursed for subscriptions to benefits to professionals from other counties. Furthermore, amateurs should be reimbursed per season for their expenditure on one bat, one pair of pads, a pair of white flannels, one shirt and a pair of boots. In addition to those expenses, the club should provide 'a round of drinks in the amateurs' dressing room at the close of play [at the Oval]'. None of that was to the taste of the MCC.

All in all, the responses of the county clubs to Aird's letter duly arrived at Lord's and were considered by a special sub-committee of the MCC. At their meeting on 13 July 1949 under the chairmanship of R. H. Twining the sub-committee noted that many of the responses from counties had been 'vague' and – with some irritation – that the term 'out of pocket expenses' was used without any details of what those expenses actually were. After much discussion they decided to recommend to the counties that ordinary travelling and hotel expenses should be paid in full, an extra twenty-five shillings per match should be paid for equipment and clothing, a further five shillings per match for tips (unless this was done by the captain on behalf of the whole team) and a special entertainment allowance for the captain for 'communal hospitality'.

That decided, the sub-committee went on to consider the thorny matter of compensation for 'broken time'. It was immediately pointed out that this was a very difficult and complex problem. In fact, it turned out to be so difficult and complex that they ducked the issue altogether. They decided to make no recommendation to the counties, not least because more than one member of the sub-committee had declared roundly that any such compensation could not possibly be called expenses and would therefore be incompatible with amateur status as hitherto understood.

That might have settled the matter of 'broken time'. But it was soon to rise to the surface again. On 31 July 1950, Colonel Rait Kerr wrote to all members of the MCC Committee informing them that Trevor Bailey had written to him to say that, unless the amateurs' expense allowance for the forthcoming Ashes tour of Australia and New Zealand was substantially increased from the £200 on offer, he could not afford to go and would therefore be unable to accept the invitation. The Committee was asked to convene for a special meeting to discuss Bailey's letter. But Rait Kerr was under no illusions. He believed that there was a concerted campaign by the amateurs, including the captain, F. R. Brown, supported by the *Evening Standard*, to force the hand of the MCC over what amounted to payment for 'broken time', and that this should be resisted.

The Committee duly deliberated. There was no question, they said, of allowing 'broken time' payments. On the other hand, as the minute of their meeting records, they 'had regard to the change in the value of money since 1939' – whatever that was supposed to mean. On that flimsy pretext the Committee raised the amount to be paid to the captain on the tour from £250 to £350 and to the other amateurs from £200 to £300 (roughly £8,000 today). In a stroke, of course, they thus destroyed the case against 'broken time' compensation for amateurs not just for Ashes tours but, as Rait Kerr pointed out, for all future overseas tours.

In the world of county cricket, such as it was in the early 1950s, many of the MCC's recommendations were routinely ignored by county committees. The clubs were, after all, independent organisations and responsible only to themselves. The MCC could only enforce rules in tours or matches in which it had its own jurisdiction. Furthermore, county committees were also amateurs themselves – with little or no sense of management beyond that which some of them had picked up in the armed forces. The result was, as in the matter of amateurs' expenses, one of confused variety. Surrey County Cricket Club, for instance, set up its own subcommittee to look at amateurs' expenses in Test matches. This arrived at conclusions far removed from those of the MCC, claiming that the term 'out of pocket expenses' was a perfectly reasonable one and that they should be met in full. There was then an irritable exchange of letters between Brian Castor, the Surrey Secretary, and Rait Kerr which resulted in no agreement – except to disagree.

The confused variety led to some sensible results. At Essex in the 1950s, for instance, our system was very simple – and informal. We amateurs were asked by our captain Doug Insole, normally at the end of each match, how much we had spent over the three days. The sum agreed, we then received cash in return. There was no question of receipts or bills – we were always believed. In fact, our expenses were never more than modest and there was no suggestion of dishonest claims. The only problem was that the system involved Insole carrying around large sums in cash, particularly for away matches, given the relatively high number of amateurs in the side.

Amateurs had no contract. They were free to come and go as they pleased. Raman Subba Row, for example, felt able to move from Surrey to Northamptonshire when he was offered the captaincy and a sinecure as Assistant Secretary. Special registration was in his case a mere formality. (He simply told Surrey that he wished to transfer.) In fact, as the 1950s wore on it became evident that there were few amateurs who did not have similarly helpful jobs. This was mostly true of county captains, who were obliged by their position to play a full season without interruption unless they were selected for Test matches. Even among those of us who were not captains (at least not of county sides) it was tempting to accept some of the offers which were made by well-wishers. In short, it was generally recognised that an amateur could not afford to play continuous county cricket living on expenses alone.

This gave rise to what became the main grievance of the professionals. Of those of us who played as amateurs not many could swear that we were not supported financially, one way or another, to allow time to play for the county of choice. In a long and mournful letter to Harry Altham, MCC President in 1956, Alec Bedser complained that amateurs were taking the 'plums' away from professionals – lending their name for advertisements, being paid as 'secretaries' or 'other official positions' when in fact all they were doing was playing cricket along with professionals.

Professionals also had a different problem. Unlike the amateurs, they, of course, had contracts. In truth, these were not elaborate legal documents. One Essex professional of the time has kept an example from 1950. It is little more than a sheet of poor-quality paper with some poor-quality typing. But it was a contract, and it did require the player to play (if selected and unless incapacitated) during the period of the contract. The main problem was that the period ran from September of one year to September of the next. At the end of the season, therefore, the player was on tenterhooks to know whether he would be renewed, and at what salary. Capped players were generally given some sort of reassurance towards the end of the season but juniors could expect no such favours. If they were not renewed they faced a particularly hard winter.

Winter was a difficult time for both seniors and juniors, at least for those who were not invited on MCC tours. Jobs were not always easy to come by. In Essex the Co-op was the most willing employer for part-time labour, but there were other local firms which would take players for temporary work. Some counties continued to pay salaries over the winter but at a reduced rate, but the general rule was that players had to settle for what they could get (working in pubs was a favourite, particularly over the busy Christmas period).

Compared with today's cricketers, the financial life of those of us who loved the game, and played it to the best of our ability, was meagre. Amateurs who were not supported with phantom jobs had to live on their own means. Professionals lived a dangerous existence, not knowing whether they would be in or out of employment the following year. Many, in fact, had to rely on the generosity of their club's members to see them through.

The truth is that first-class cricket in the 1950s was still an amateur business. The MCC was (and still is) a members' club, as were all the counties. Moreover, the clubs were always short of money. In the days before handsome television revenues came in to rescue the game's finances clubs were doing no better than scraping along.

There were, of course, various devices to bolster clubs' balance sheets. The favourite was to appeal to members for supplements to the annual membership subscription. Another device was to run a football pool. The most successful was run by Warwickshire, with Glamorgan the next most successful. In Essex the pool was managed by the senior professional of the day (also Secretary of the Supporters' Association – which helped to supplement his income). For one shilling the punters were invited to mark their cards with their prediction of the results of various football matches. Of that shilling twopence went to the county cricket club and tenpence went into the pool, to be paid out to the winner. The Essex pool was unfortunately not particularly successful (not least because a group of committee members objected on Christian grounds to 'gambling') but Warwickshire and Glamorgan, largely because of their urban hinterlands of Birmingham and Cardiff, were both able to accumulate so much cash that they were able to lend money on favourable terms to other clubs which were struggling. (In fact, Essex was a beneficiary of this largesse. Trevor Bailey negotiated a loan from Warwickshire to allow the club to purchase what is now the county ground at Chelmsford.)

All in all, and in retrospect, it is surprising that so many county clubs survived the 1950s. There were, to be sure, rumours from time to time of financial problems but members always seemed to come to the rescue. Yet it was never healthy, and the stresses on county finances started to affect the continuing dispute over the payment to amateurs off 'the cricket field'. As Alec Bedser had pointed out, the amateurs were taking all the 'plums', and the professionals did not like it. He for one would much prefer there to be no such thing as 'amateur and professional' but all to be just 'players'. His view, as it happened, ran directly contrary to the view expressed at a meeting of the Amateur Status Sub-Committee of the MCC in February of the same year that the object in discussing the question at all was to consider 'how more amateur players could be enabled to play in first class cricket'. The controversy was coming to the boil – and the boiling pot would soon land in the capacious lap of the new President of the MCC, no less a figure than the Earl Marshal of England, Bernard, the 16th Duke of Norfolk.

7

THE DUKE'S MEN

'The biggest lot of poppycock I have heard'

Bernard Marmaduke Fitzalan-Howard KG GCVO GBE TD PC, Earl Marshal, Chief Butler of England, the 16th Duke of Norfolk, was by any standards the most aristocratic of aristocrats. He was also, as it happened, devoted to the game of cricket. The facts of his life are, to be sure, not unduly complicated. Born into the Roman Catholic purple, he was brought up in the great traditions of his family. His childhood was in the daunting surroundings of Arundel Castle (as soon as he was born he became Earl of Arundel and Surrey). At the age of nine his father died and he assumed the title of Duke of Norfolk together with its attendant subsidiary titles, as well as the hereditary position of Earl Marshal of England. Educated at The Oratory School – in the strictest Catholic discipline – he was not considered to be university material and was steered towards the Army. Commissioned into the Royal Horse Guards at the age of twenty-three he did not find military life to his taste and resigned his commission only two years later. He fought in the Second World War as a major and was wounded in action. Before the war he had played his part in the Coronation of King George VI and after the war played a similar part in the Coronation of Queen Elizabeth, the investiture of the Prince of Wales at Carnarvon Castle and, later, the funeral of Sir Winston Churchill. Apart from his official duties and the management of his large estate, Duke Bernard lent his name and time to a variety of charities. In short, he was the very model of a (more or less) modern Duke of Norfolk.

To meet, Duke Bernard was a kindly soul and, when he climbed down from the heights of his dukedom, an affable and jovial enough companion. It would be wrong, of course, to suppose that he was ever a 'man of the people'. A natural conservative in politics, as in everything else, he took little part in the proceedings of the House of Lords. Nevertheless, he was a conscientious (if old-fashioned) landlord and always tried to do what he thought was the right thing. (In the 1955 General Election, for instance, he took the trouble to ask Conservative Central Office 'how he should tell his tenants to vote'.) Therefore, when the MCC were undecided who should manage the team for the Ashes tour of 1962–3, at the drinks party after the Committee meeting Duke Bernard thought that it would be the right thing to do to put his hand up. He casually said that if nobody else wanted the job he would be quite happy to volunteer. Much to the general surprise, his suggestion was immediately accepted. Behind the scenes, it seemed to have been agreed that he would be the only person who would be able to control the new and turbulent England captain, Ted Dexter.

Although he had long been a member of the MCC Committee, Duke Bernard could never be described as an expert at the game. When he played at the Arundel ground, which his father had constructed, he is said to have made sure that his own butler was standing as umpire, with the consequent verdict on any appeal against him being decided in favour of the Duke when batting and in favour of the Duke when bowling. There apparently was no question of the Duke being out first ball and even when he was palpably out thereafter the butler was obliged to announce that 'His Grace is not in'.

Given all this, for the Ashes tour of 1962–3 the MCC sensibly decided to appoint an experienced cricketer as Assistant Manager to the Duke. The mantle duly fell on Alec Bedser. It turned out to be a wise choice. When the touring party arrived in Australia in late 1962, Duke Bernard, by then portly and florid of face, announced that he wished it to be an informal tour – and that the Australians should therefore only address him as 'sir' rather than 'Your Grace'. The response of the Australian press was one of incredulous hilarity. To his team he was at times formal – on occasions to be addressed as 'Your Grace' – and at times informal – in the communal bath they were allowed to call him 'Bernard'.

The tour got off to a difficult start at the first press conference. The questions were not about the cricket to come but whether Duke Bernard's horses would be racing in Australia and, in particular, whether his favourite jockey, Scobie Breasley, would be flying out to ride for him. After that, much of the popular attention was focused on the Duke's horses and where they would be running. It was, as Ted Dexter tells it, left to Alec Bedser to do the managing of the cricket team. Duke Bernard did the 'socialising'.

In fact, the only managing Duke Bernard did, according to Dexter, was to offer to lend his sleeping pills to a fellow insomniac on the tour, Ken Barrington.

When Duke Bernard became President of the MCC in early October 1957 he found that the most pressing problem was the status of amateurs in the first-class game. A committee had been set up in December 1955 under the Presidency of Field Marshal Earl Alexander of Tunis to study the matter but it had only met sporadically and reached no conclusions other than to recommend, in its meeting of 28 February 1956, that a special sub-committee be set up to study the whole framework of first-class cricket. Needless to say the suggestion was not immediately followed up and lay for a time on the table.

But the question of amateurism became rather more urgent with a report from Freddie Brown on the 1956–7 MCC tour of South Africa. Brown had any number of conversations with both amateurs and professionals on the tour about amateur status and reported that many amateurs felt that overseas tours were becoming too expensive. The professionals, on the other hand, felt that amateurs were enjoying too much largesse at their expense and wanted all tourists to be on the same financial footing. When this came to the attention of the MCC Committee they decided that the Sub-Committee should indeed be relaunched as a Special Sub-Committee to be asked specifically to conduct an in-depth enquiry into amateur status and to produce a report. The start of the enquiry was fixed to coincide with the arrival of Duke Bernard as President of the MCC.

For the relaunch, it was necessary to bolster the

membership of the Sub-Committee. Of the earlier Committee, Gubby Allen (of course), Maurice Allom (another old-stager), Peter May and Charles Palmer stayed on, but Duke Bernard sought to have greater representation from the counties, and Geoffrey Howard from Lancashire, Brian Sellers from Yorkshire, Desmond Eagar from Hampshire, Doug Insole from Essex and David Sheppard from Sussex were all drafted in. The MCC retained two voting places – Duke Bernard himself and the Treasurer (Harry Altham), with the Secretary and the Assistant Secretary in attendance. All the Duke's men, it goes without saying, were amateurs.

As with all committees, some voices turned out to be stronger than others. Of the fifteen voting members (including Duke Bernard) the most vociferous, and hence the most influential, were, in no particular order, Harry Altham, Gubby Allen, Freddie Brown, Doug Insole, Peter May (not least because he was the current England captain), Rowan Rait Kerr, Brian Sellers and David Sheppard. Others, such as Desmond Eagar, Maurice Allom and Charles Palmer, chipped in from time to time, but their appearance in the minutes of meetings is very much less frequent than that of the others.

Of the leading characters, Allen talked the most but Altham was probably the most influential. He was, after all, the sitting MCC Treasurer and had been Chairman of selectors in 1954; his words carried corresponding weight. Stocky, soft-spoken with the classic voice of a Winchester schoolmaster, he was much liked as well as respected. In fact, it is difficult to recall anybody who took against him. He was particularly good, in a fatherly kind of way, with professionals, most of whom (Jim Laker was an obvious exception) were rather in awe of him.

Altham's playing career had been interrupted by service in the First World War. From Repton he had gone on to Oxford and won his Blue in 1911 and 1912 as a right-handed bat and a bowler of medium pace. He then had a successful war – Distinguished Service Order, Military Cross and Mentioned in Despatches three times – before joining the staff at Winchester College, where he stayed throughout his career of thirty years. Not the least of his achievements was a history of cricket produced with E. W. ('Jim') Swanton in 1962. As one of the critics put it, the book is written with 'authority and affection, accuracy and charm'.

Brian Sellers was almost the direct opposite. Where Altham was quite patently a southerner, Sellers was Yorkshire through and through. Where Altham was clearly a public school and Oxford product, Sellers was state-educated and regarded himself as a living example of northern grit – and his accent showed it. Neither of them were outstanding batsmen but Sellers was probably just the better of the two. What he was good at, however, was captaincy. Appointed captain of Yorkshire in 1933 at the age twenty-six, he won the championship six times in a total of ten seasons in post, making him the third most successful county captain ever (after Lord Hawke and Stuart Surridge).

In fact, his captaincy started badly. He had been pushed into the job by the Yorkshire committee – his father was a member – and had difficulty in asserting himself in what he regarded as his proper role. He was consistently (and unnecessarily) loud-mouthed when dealing with professionals, insisted that when they addressed amateurs it should always be as 'Mr' – and then the surname – and they should expect amateurs to address them by their surname alone. He also went out of his way to impose a fierce discipline. For instance, he laid down a rule that all players should be at the ground one hour before the start of play. On one occasion Len Hutton, having just played in a Test match, turned up only half an hour before the start. Thinking that his sin would be pardoned because of his Test appearance he put on his pads ready to open the batting, only for Sellers to remark brutally that 'it was the first time he had seen a twelfth man with his pads on'.

It was not long before the Yorkshire professionals became so disenchanted that they decided, at the prompting of Herbert Sutcliffe, the senior professional, to play a trick. One morning when Yorkshire were in the field they let Sellers walk in stately manner, as the only amateur, out of the amateurs' gate while they stayed in the pavilion. For some minutes Sellers was left alone with the two umpires before Sutcliffe led the professionals out through their gate. The ensuing language, laced as it was with the most basic profanities, was apparently a wonder to hear. But Sellers never changed his ways. As a matter of fact, even when he retired from the captaincy in 1948, Sellers would not let go. He went to every home match, sat watching in the committee room and was very free with his comments to any player who offended him.

David Sheppard was one of the group of great Cambridge University batsmen of the early 1950s. In 1952, in fact, he headed the overall first-class batting averages with an almost unprecedented figure for an undergraduate of 64.62. It was also at Cambridge that he discovered his vocation to become a priest and, after studying at Ridley Hall, he was ordained in 1955. Retiring from cricket to pursue his career in the Church, Sheppard was abruptly recalled in 1956 to play in the Fourth Ashes Test against Australia (known as 'Laker's Test' since he took 19 out of 20 wickets) and made a sparkling 113 in England's only innings.

Sheppard then joined the Mayflower mission in the East End of London but he agreed, after consulting the then Archbishop of Canterbury, Geoffrey Fisher, to come out of retirement again for Duke Bernard's Ashes tour of 1962–3. It was a way, the Archbishop opined, to spread the word of God more widely in the southern hemi-sphere. But apart from making 113 in the second Test at Melbourne, Sheppard had an unsuccessful tour, in par-ticular dropping a number of vital catches. Trueman was heard to tell him, after yet another dropped catch off his bowling, to 'pretend it's Sunday, Reverend, and keep your hands together'. One Australian wag invented the story that Sheppard was asked to be godfather to a baby but that Mrs Sheppard advised against it on the grounds that 'he was sure to drop it'. For all that, Sheppard preached in the Anglican cathedrals of every state capital from Perth to Brisbane and filled them to the doors.

Although he could rightly claim to be the only ordained priest to have played Test cricket, Sheppard was, while undoubtedly sincere in his Christianity, competitive in his playing and, occasionally, sharp-tongued as a captain. Those of us who got to know him well as a cricketer found him somewhat brusque but in his later years in the House of Lords he had mellowed almost to serenity. Yet there is little doubt that Duke Bernard, for all their joint Sussex connections, found him a touch prickly.

In preparation for the first meeting of the Special Sub-Committee on 9 October 1957 there had been three papers. Rait Kerr had produced a paper outlining the brief of the Sub-Committee and drawing attention to the reasons for the enquiry. Gubby Allen could not be restrained from producing a second paper extolling the virtues of amateurs in cricket. Sheppard, on the other hand, took a contrary view, putting forward the opinion (in terms agreeable to evangelical Christianity) that all men should be treated equally and that the distinction between amateur and professional should be abolished.

In addition to these papers, Duke Bernard had decided to put forward his own views. In a memorandum written at Arundel on 26 August 1957 he said that he had read and reread the 'interesting' papers on amateur status. He then proceeded to outline his own position. Genuine amateurs, he wrote, should be encouraged as 'they usually have a better outlook on the game and the social side which does play a part'. The professional, he went on, had 'every right to be given his chance to play cricket' and 'there must never be a question of him being left out because it is cheaper to play an amateur ... the professional must never be able to make the charge of hypocrisy'. Furthermore, he added, there was a 'very real relationship between the amateur and the professional which I believe is very strong'.

Duke Bernard's memorandum set the tone for the

deliberations of the Special Sub-Committee. The dice, in other words, were loaded at the start in favour of the status quo of amateurism. At the outset of the first meeting of the reconstituted Sub-Committee on 9 October 1957, Gubby Allen, as the author of one of the preparatory papers, was called on first. After the preliminaries – Duke Bernard thanking the attendance and those who had contributed the first papers, stressing the need for confidentiality and requesting a recital of the Sub-Committee's brief – Allen set out his stall. It was vital, he said, that a niche was left in the game for the amateur, and he, for one, would never support the amateur's abolition. After all, the three best batsmen in the country and the only all-rounder were amateurs and vital to the composition of any England side. David Sheppard, who followed Allen, was much more restrained. As he said afterwards, he realised that the tide was flowing against him and, rather than immediately arguing for an out-and-out abolition of the distinction between amateur and professional he contented himself with urging the Sub-Committee not to rush to any decision before all the options had been examined.

There followed a general discussion, with Duke Bernard inviting each member to outline his views. All agreed that there were two distinct problems: the position of the amateur at home and the position of the amateur on tour. Furthermore, all agreed, in what became a rather rambling discussion, that the MCC should be able to send the most gifted cricketers on the major tours regardless of their status and that therefore amateurs 'on tour should receive some form of financial aid'. The matter of how this could be done was left over for future deliberation.

Before the meeting concluded it was agreed that 'certain cricketers' (in other words professionals) would be useful to help their efforts. Duke Bernard, Rait Kerr, Insole and the new Secretary of the MCC, Ronald Aird, were charged with selecting the future participants.

At the next meeting of the Sub-Committee three weeks later, on 31 October 1957, opinions were hardening. But the discussion again wandered. After agreement that the financial aid which amateurs should be entitled to claim when on tour should take the form of 'broken time' payments, there was a spirited argument about 'irregularities' in the domestic game. Aird quickly pointed out that the MCC had no jurisdiction over county clubs on 'broken time' payments to amateurs playing in the domestic game – it was entirely up to them what they wished to do. That said, Allen and Sheppard both returned to the attack. Allen felt that the abolition of amateur status would be a 'feeble line to take' and that it was essential to maintain the distinction between the player who worked at some other occupation and the 'amateur' who made cricket 'his profession entirely'. Duke Bernard then intervened to state his view that there were, and always would be, cricketers who wished to play as true amateurs and that the position of those players should be protected.

Nothing daunted, Sheppard came out in his full colours. The only logical step, he argued, was the abolition altogether of the distinction between amateur and professional. He emphatically rejected the idea (put forward earlier by Maurice Allom) that amateurs under a new dispensation would somehow have reduced social status. Allen responded by claiming that if all the amateurs were to become professional they would have to cease their membership of the MCC. Sheppard replied that the MCC was already losing the effectiveness of committees such as this by excluding professionals. Allom chipped in to say that the assistant secretary of a county club who did little or no work as such was the chief transgressor. At that point there was a good deal of nodding of heads, although Freddie Brown insisted that the money for an assistant secretary was sometimes put up by a friendly local firm (he was thinking, no doubt, of British Timken at Northampton) which was very difficult to monitor.

That was the sharpest exchange in any session of the Special Sub-Committee. But Duke Bernard calmed them down, tempers then cooled, and the business moved on. There was a nervous moment when Allen raised the doubt that the Sub-Committee might be wasting its time if the county clubs were not disposed to accept its recommendations. Duke Bernard and Aird both stepped in to remind members that most of the counties had agreed to the MCC carrying out this examination. Attention then focused on the team of professionals who were to be invited to meet a small number of members of the Sub-Committee (Duke Bernard, Rowan Rait Kerr, Doug Insole, Gubby Allen and Maurice Allom). After some debate, the list was decided: Alec Bedser, Godfrey Evans, Les Ames, Tom Dollery, Cyril Washbrook and David Smith. The meeting was then fixed for 15 November at Lord's (there was no suggestion that the chosen professionals might decide not to make themselves available).

The meeting with the six professionals duly took place. But it was not an altogether easy occasion. Duke Bernard started off by reminding them that any discussion which took place was entirely confidential. (The warning, like other similar previous warnings, was effective, in that no one outside the magic circle had any idea that the meeting was taking place – or, for that matter, that there was an MCC Sub-Committee meeting for the purpose at all.) He went on to stress that nothing must be done to disturb the 'very special and wonderful relationship' which had always existed between the amateur and the professional in cricket. As might be imagined, among the attendant professionals a few eyebrows were raised.

The meeting then turned to the substance of the matter. There were several points, in fact, which were vexing the professionals. Their expenses on tour, they considered, should be on the same basis as amateurs' expenses – the same amount and equally tax-free. Rait Kerr pointed out correctly that the exemption from tax was beyond the MCC's power to deliver. Les Ames focused next on the anomaly of amateur captains and assistant secretaries who were in many cases paid more than professionals. Alec Bedser objected to the practice of amateurs signing bats for a fee and engaging in various forms of advertising. Cyril Washbrook claimed that the main bone of contention was 'shamateurism' – particularly the point that Ames had made. Moving on to the subject of overseas tours, there was unanimous professional opposition to 'broken time' payments for amateurs on tours. Nevertheless, at the end of the meeting all were in agreement that the amateur should continue to play his part. Alec Bedser even went on to say that he personally liked to see amateurs captaining county sides – provided they were genuine amateurs.

On that note of comparative harmony the meeting broke up.

The result of the meeting was duly conveyed to the third plenary session of the Sub-Committee on 28 November 1957. Opening the session, Duke Bernard, surprisingly in view of the frank arguments which had taken place, told members that he thought some had been too shy (or too reverential) to express their views fully. He reminded them that not only were the discussions entirely confidential but also that their job was only to report to the MCC who, in turn, might put proposals to the county clubs which they would be free to accept or reject. To encourage members to be more forthright, he assured them that he would publish, if asked, the names of any dissenters from any recommendations that were made and that he would even consider publishing a minority report.

Duke Bernard no doubt spoke in good faith. But the result was effectively to silence any opposition for fear of disloyalty. When he went on to say that the time had come to go further in their deliberations, namely to take a decision on a recommendation about the fundamental issue – whether or not the present distinction between amateurs and professionals should continue – the effect of the Duke's initial intervention became clear. Since David Sheppard (the only articulate opponent) was unable to be present, the debate, such as it was, turned out to be one-sided and lasted only a few minutes. Duke Bernard then called for a vote on the proposal that 'the distinctive status of the amateur cricketer should be preserved as in the opinion of the Sub-Committee this was not obsolete and was of great value to the game'. The proposal, it need hardly be said, was approved unanimously.

That done (with a certain amount of self-congratulation), the meeting went on to consider the various anomalies which had been identified. The matter of 'shamateurism' was addressed – somewhat on tiptoe. Insole pointed out that it would be very difficult to enforce a rule about pseudo-'Assistant Secretaries'. Rait Kerr agreed and said that all the Sub-Committee could properly do was to 'deplore certain practices'. Charles Palmer proposed that any amateur directly or indirectly paid for playing cricket by a county cricket club or any associated organisation should be regarded as a professional. This was agreed (without anybody having a clear idea of how it might be enforced). It was further agreed that there should be an independent committee of arbitration set up to adjudicate cases and reporting to the standing committee of county chairmen and secretaries, the Advisory County Cricket Committee (ACCC).

They then addressed the matter of amateurs engaging in advertising. This was to be allowed, subject to the rules drawn up by the MCC for home Test matches and by county committees for their own players. (The possibility that those paying for advertising might be an 'associated organisation' seemingly passed them by.) Lastly, they went on to the matter of 'broken time' for those amateurs who were losing money from their employment as a result of going on tour. Rait Kerr reported that some of the professionals who had been interviewed had now changed their minds and would agree that there was a case in favour – provided the MCC made full enquiry on each circumstance. On the proposal of Rait Kerr, it was agreed that the principle of 'broken time' for overseas tours should be agreed, but that the meaning of 'broken time' should be clearly defined as the 'loss of earnings during the winter period' and that if 'broken time' were paid there should be strict limit to amateurs' expenses. On that reasonably happy note the Sub-Committee broke up, agreeing to a further meeting on the last day of 1957 to consider a draft report.

Before they left, however, Duke Bernard sounded a somewhat ominous note. The professionals who had been interviewed had recorded a change of attitude in the younger professionals who were coming into the first-class game. They seemed to think that amateurs were something of an obsolete species and, as such, not deserving respect. The senior professionals, brought up as they were in the old traditions of the game, regretted this, but it was a matter which had to be addressed. He very much hoped that the result of the deliberations of the Sub-Committee would be to increase the respect of young professionals for the amateur and 'the position restored'.

The fourth meeting of the Sub-Committee, on 31 December 1957, was short. A draft Report was presented – largely written by Rait Kerr – and members were invited to take it away and submit any amendments they wished to make in good time for the next meeting, which was fixed for 15 January. Duke Bernard then reminded them all of the confidential nature of the proceedings and that the report, in its final version, would not be published until it had been approved by the full MCC Committee and the ACCC at their next meeting.

New Year 1958 came and went. When the Sub-Committee reconvened at Lord's for its fifth – and last – meeting they found that, in all, eleven amendments to the draft Report had been tabled. In truth, only three were of substance. The first was designed to ensure that all players on overseas tours, amateurs and professionals, were treated equally in the matter of expenses. The second emphasised the principle that the MCC should always field the strongest possible side on overseas tours and that amateurs should be paid to make good any financial loss they suffered because of their participation. The third, and most controversial, amendment was to ensure that payments to amateurs on MCC tours should be substantially below the salaries of the professionals. Quite what 'substantially' meant was a matter of some debate. It was suggested that a figure of 50 per cent should be in the Report itself, but the general mood was that this would be a mistake. As a compromise, it was agreed that such a figure should be put in the covering letter to county clubs accompanying the Report when it was sent out. It only remained for Duke Bernard to thank members for their attendance and to wish them a happy New Year. They in turn dutifully thanked Duke Bernard for his chairmanship and went their several ways.

The final Report was signed off by Duke Bernard and Aird on 14 February 1958. It was duly approved with commendable speed by the MCC Committee and the ACCC and published on the 18th. As a document, the Report can hardly be said to be a masterpiece of the English language. Nor, for that matter, does it deviate much from the views set out at its origin by Duke Bernard. In its preamble, the Report emphasised 'the wish to preserve in first class cricket the leadership and general approach to the game traditionally associated with the Amateur player'. Moreover, 'the leading Amateurs [should not] be prevented by the hard facts of present day economics from accepting invitations to accompany major MCC touring teams'. That said, the Report goes on to reject 'any solution of the problem on the lines of abolishing the distinction between Amateur and Professional and regarding them all alike as "cricketers" ... The distinctive status of the amateur cricketer was not obsolete, was of great value to the game and should be preserved.' There was, of course, the matter of defining what constituted amateur status. Here the Report sounds a less certain note. Any cricketer carrying out full-time administrative duties with a county club was to continue to be regarded as an amateur. On the other hand, any cricketer directly or indirectly paid for '*playing* cricket' (the word 'playing' is in italics in the text of the Report) by a county cricket club or any associated organisation should be regarded as a professional. After that firm statement the Report wobbles. The problem of the pseudo-'Assistant Secretary' who might in fact be paid for playing cricket under the umbrella of his nominal secretarial duties was deemed to be impossible for general solution and was left to the counties to sort out. The associated problem of friendly commercial firms who paid amateurs a salary on the clear understanding that they would be playing cricket all summer and, in some cases, most of the winter, was ignored altogether. On that matter, the Report remains – as had the Sub-Committee itself in its deliberations – silent.

The Report goes on to deal with advertising, writing and broadcasting. This was not too difficult. No restrictions on amateurs were suggested other than those imposed by the MCC on official overseas tours. Appearing by amateurs on advertisements was a bit more difficult (the professionals had complained about this) but was to be allowed – 'subject to review from time to time'. Amateurs' expenses and allowances was a much bigger problem. Generally, the Report stated that 'expense allowances must be restricted to those expenses actually incurred during a match, including meals during travelling and gratuities, with an additional amount to cover special cost of laundry and of the upkeep of cricket equipment'.

That was all very well. But nobody could come up with any sort of formula to apply the principle of 'an additional amount' in practice. The best they could do was to invite the ACCC to give urgent consideration to this matter with a view to establishing a formula for such allowances. (There is no evidence that this ever happened. Certainly, one amateur – C. C. P. Williams – was wholly unaware of any formula and never received any help with replacing his dilapidated pads.) To complete their recommendations, and after long debate, the Sub-Committee agreed in the Report to 'broken time' for 'major MCC overseas tours'. Amateurs would have to make an application for compensation for loss of earnings but in all cases any such compensation should be 'substantially' below the payment made to professionals on any tour. But no figure was put on 'substantially' and nobody was clear on how it would work out.

The Sub-Committee had one final bullet to fire. It

recommended that 'the MCC should inform the ACCC
that, if invited, they would set up a Standing Committee
to examine and report on any doubtful case of status'. In
other words, there would be a committee of amateurs to
investigate the position of other amateurs still playing the
game who might or might not be in receipt of any 'payment, including expenses, made directly or indirectly ...
by a County Club or any associated organisation'. But one
feature of the Standing Committee which was to investigate us was reminiscent of the Soviet Union. 'Reports of
the Standing Committee', the Report went on, 'shall at all
times remain confidential.' We were all, it seemed, to be
investigated in confidence – even those of us who did no
more than ask to be reimbursed for what we had spent.

The Special Sub-Committee's duly published Report
was on 18 February 1958. It was immediately branded,
not least by the *Daily Express*, as 'the Great Whitewash,
or the Shamateurs' Charter'. Some newspapers, however,
were less unkind. *The Times*, for example, recognised that
the Report was 'bound to meet with certain criticisms ...
some will say that the line drawn between the amateur and
the professional is now so slight that it might as well not
exist ... it was not a straightforward problem, and had the
MCC not made some attempt to tackle it they would, as
the Duke of Norfolk said, have been failing in their duty
to cricket'. Other newspapers followed more or less the
same line. Yet after the Report had been approved, on
12 March, by the Advisory County Cricket Committee,
Jim Laker reflected the views of many professionals when,
at a meeting of the Cricket Society the following day, he
declared that 'a cricketer who cannot afford to play as

an amateur either should not play or should become a professional ... broken time payments for amateurs on tour [were] the biggest lot of poppycock I have heard. An amateur can make more money on the side than a professional.'

Duke Bernard's Special Sub-Committee had thus come to its less than glorious end. The Advisory County Cricket Committee did indeed ask the MCC to set up yet another Standing Committee to investigate us amateurs. This was duly done and approved by the full MCC Committee. So it was that an old-fashioned members' club (of amateurs), without any proper legal powers and against the grain of the times, set out to control the habits – and livelihoods – of individuals who wished, in most cases, to enjoy the game they loved. It is hardly surprising that the endeavour failed. Before that happened, however, there were some unpleasant exchanges between the new Standing Committee and the county clubs. The 'Star Chamber', as it came to be called, had started its work.

8

THE 'STAR CHAMBER'

'... this ridiculous state of affairs'

By the early spring of 1958 the MCC had landed itself with no fewer than four committees in pursuit of what was proving to be a very elusive hare. First, there was the MCC Committee itself. Then there was Duke Bernard's Special Sub-Committee on Amateur Status, which was still to meet from time to time (now calling itself the Special Committee, without the 'Sub'). That, in turn, had spawned the Amateur Status Standing Committee which was to do the dirty work of chasing the hare to ground. Finally, there was the Advisory County Cricket Committee of county club secretaries, which, although formally agreeing with what the other committees were doing, persisted in sniping at them from the sidelines. It is hardly surprising that the whole thing gave rise to a great deal of confusion and bad temper which, in the end, led directly to the final abandonment of what had hitherto been, for the MCC and its attendant committees, the search for the ultimate prize – a settled form of amateur status for first-class cricket.

The Amateur Status Standing Committee met for the

first time on 16 April 1958. The meeting started badly. Duke Bernard's Special Committee had left them with only the vaguest of terms of reference. They were 'to be empowered to examine any case of payment, including expenses, made directly or indirectly to an Amateur by a County Club or any associated organisation'. Nowadays, of course, such a brief would have been dismissed by any court without argument on the grounds that a members' club had no right to investigate such matters in the case of those who were not its members. But by good fortune – or perhaps hitherto unsuspected good judgement – the MCC had found almost the perfect Chairman for the new committee, able to smooth over the difficulties of procedure and practice which would certainly be involved. Among all the illogicalities this was at least one shining piece of logic – that the main drafter of the final Report of Duke Bernard's Committee, Rowan Rait Kerr, should himself take centre stage as the enforcer of its conclusions.

It was a good choice for what would turn out to be a most unpleasant task. Rait Kerr was one of the most benign of men – he was, as it were, everybody's favourite uncle. Born in Ireland in 1891, he went to Sandhurst, had a distinguished First World War (Military Cross in 1916) and been Secretary of the MCC (on the back of six matches accepted – dubiously – as first class before the Second World War) from 1936 to 1952. Quietly spoken yet firm in his views, he had a great love of the game of cricket but also a sense that it must be seen to be honourable. Both these qualities were to be exercised to the utmost in the two and a half years which followed his appointment as Chairman of the Standing Committee.

Rait Kerr's colleagues on the Standing Committee were, to be honest, of little help in what was to become a gruelling task. Maurice Allom and Cyril Hastilow had served on Duke Bernard's Committee but they were both getting on in years and in cricketing terms were products of the period immediately after the First World War – and even then only on the fringes of the first-class game. The same could be said of George Shelmerdine, another old sweat from the same period and equally on the edges of the game. George Mann was a more substantial figure – he had captained Middlesex and England after the Second World War, until 1949, when he decided that his responsibilities to his family brewery took precedence and he retired. Making up this (not very impressive) team was Ronald Aird, Rait Kerr's successor as MCC Secretary, and his Assistant Secretary, the urbane, and perhaps a little bit too smooth, figure of Jim Dunbar.

At their first meeting Rait Kerr went out of his way to explain to the Standing Committee the genesis of their existence and their terms of reference. These were, he said, set out in the Report of Duke Bernard's Committee. The whole thing, he explained, was to be completely confidential. The 'rules of procedure', to be approved by the full MCC Committee, should provide for a complete list of all amateurs playing for counties during the 1958 season together with details of how they were treated financially. After all that had been received and digested, the Standing Committee would then proceed to investigate those cases which seemed *prima facie* dubious. The Committee then addressed the matter of what was right and proper for amateurs to receive by way of expenses – without any substantive conclusion. The only firm decision was that county clubs should be told about the existence of the Standing Committee (confidentially, of course) and asked for their list of amateur players.

This proposal ran into trouble from the start. A draft letter to give effect to it was considered at the next meeting of the Standing Committee on 29 April. Allom and Hastilow questioned the wisdom of asking counties to submit the names of all their amateur players. It would be better, they thought, to confine the enquiry to those amateurs who were receiving payment in addition to 'out of pocket expenses'. In the light of the obvious dispute, Rait Kerr suggested that the case should be referred to the Advisory County Cricket Committee – without any recommendation.

This particular hurdle was soon jumped by Aird and Dunbar. They put the matter to the MCC Committee which agreed to do whatever they decided. Accordingly, Aird, without further reference to the Standing Committee, wrote to the county clubs on 7 May 1958. He recognised that the task was difficult but pointed out that, in the light of the unanimous acceptance by the clubs of Duke Bernard's Report, the Standing Committee had every right to expect their full cooperation. That said, they were requested to supply a list of cricketers on their registration for the 1958 season who were either amateurs employed directly by the county club or amateurs 'who receive financial assistance from any body associated with the County Club, or from any firm under a financial arrangement with the County Club or with any body associated with the County Club'.

The language was suitably slippery – in fact, fatally so. It allowed county clubs to ignore financial 'assistance' given to players by firms which employed them and paid them directly without engaging in any 'financial arrangement' with the county club itself. Aird had recognised that the MCC had no right at all to request that information. As the responses to his letter came in, it became clear that county clubs had taken full advantage of this loophole. The list of amateurs in either category was in every case thus correspondingly short – in fact, it consisted only of secretaries and assistant secretaries. In Essex, for instance, although we had five amateurs on the registered list for 1958 (J. A. Bailey, T. E. Bailey, A. Hurd, D. J. Insole, C. C. P. Williams), the club was able to claim that only one name, Trevor Bailey, fell into either category. Moreover, the club could reasonably point out that Trevor Bailey, when he was not playing cricket, carried out all the tasks of a club secretary on a full-time basis. (The fact that he was playing cricket most of the year round, either for the county or on MCC tours, was not mentioned.)

Not content with leaving matters to the Standing Committee, Duke Bernard's Special Committee met on 25 June to tie up some of the loose ends from their original Report. They decided that amateurs should not receive 'testimonials' other than in respect of administrative services to a club over a period of years – and then only if organised by the club itself with a limit on individual donations. The Committee went on to tread further on the Standing Committee's ground – recommending that appeals from Standing Committee decisions on individual cases should be heard by a tribunal appointed by the Advisory County Cricket Committee. They then issued an addendum to their original Report with their conclusions.

By that time nobody was at all clear about who was meant to do what. Nevertheless, albeit in a mood of some irritation, the Standing Committee proceeded to consider the responses to the Aird letter at a meeting on 30 July. They identified three cases where amateur status was in doubt, in other words where players were remunerated other than for what were clear and established administrative duties with their county clubs. The 'special cases', as they were called, were Raman Subba Row of Northamptonshire, Donald Carr of Derbyshire and Peter Richardson of Worcestershire. In fact, it was not a matter of dealing with mere journeymen. All three were fine players in their own right – for England as well as for their counties. As it happened, all three were nominated in various years as one of *Wisden*'s Five Cricketers of the Year.

Subba Row, the first 'special case', had been born in Streatham in south London in 1932. His Indian father had migrated to Dublin just before the First World War, had studied law at Dublin university, had been called to the Irish Bar but had then moved to London and married an English girl. It was a cricketing family and Subba Row was given all the childhood encouragement he needed by his father and elder brother, at his Croydon preparatory school and, in his later youth, at Whitgift public school.

Cambridge followed – a Blue in his first year, 1951. He played as an all-rounder, bowling a mixture of leg breaks and googlies and batting in the middle order.

As his bowling became less effective (and more erratic), his batting flourished. By 1953 he was heading the Cambridge averages with 52.05 and already playing for Surrey in the vacation. By the end of the season he had scored 1,823 runs in first-class cricket, had come fifth in the national batting averages and had been selected to tour India in the winter with a Commonwealth side. That was a high point in his early career. The following season he strained a thigh muscle badly and lost form. He was even thinking of giving up the game when he received the approach from Northamptonshire. Once settled there, however, his form recovered. He came third in the national batting averages with 1,820 runs, including a treble century against his old county, Surrey, at the Oval. As a result he was selected for England against New Zealand at Manchester in July and, in spite of failure there, for the Ashes tour of 1958–9. But it was not a happy tour for him, since a broken thumb kept him out of action for a protracted period. Once back in England, however, he regained health and form and regained his place high in the national batting averages.

As batsman, Subba Row was far from orthodox. He was not athletic in the usual sense – he walked slowly with a pronounced hunchback and his legs seemed at times to be too long for his body. Like many left-handers, his strength was on the on side but he was a placer rather than a hitter of the ball. Later in his career he became more adventurous in his off-side strokes but still relied overall on deflections to leg and quickly taken runs. Surprisingly, given his physique, he was adept at quick singles; his score seemed somehow to keep pace with more robust partners without anybody noticing. To fielders this could be mildly irritating but any irritation was mitigated by a charming smile and a friendly word. Unlike many cricketers of the day (and of this) he had both a quiet personality and perfect manners.

Subba Row moved from Surrey to Northamptonshire in early 1955 in the expectation of taking over the captaincy. The club had found him a position with a local firm of accountants where he could study to become a chartered secretary and be free to play cricket both for the county and, if occasion demanded, for England. Having originally thought that he was exempt from National Service he was soon told firmly that that was not the case and that he was required to spend the years of 1956 and 1957 in the armed forces. He duly served his time in the Royal Air Force. When he came out he found that his position with the firm of accountants was no longer available. The club stepped immediately up to the mark, found him a job with a friendly local firm by the name of Noel Gay (Musical Publications) Ltd and signed a five-year agreement to pay him £1,000 a year for five years 'to cover compensation for loss of earnings, accommodation expenses while living in Northampton, travelling expenses, hotels and meals, up-keep of clothing and equipment, Captain's allowance for entertainment and tips'.

There was a good deal of clucking in the Amateur Status Standing Committee at this obvious breach of the 'broken time' rule set out by Duke Bernard's Committee and endorsed both by the Advisory County Cricket Committee and the full MCC Committee. Furthermore, the transgression became even more apparent when the Northamptonshire Secretary revealed to Aird that 'the sum agreed as compensation for loss of earnings [from Noel Gay] was, in the first place, £450'. It was the first notice the Standing Committee had received of a specific sum in payment of 'broken time'.

At the meeting of the Standing Committee on 29 October 1958 it was unanimously agreed that Subba Row did not qualify for amateur status and that Northamptonshire County Cricket Club should be so notified. Nevertheless, since there was a contract in existence, there should be a moratorium of one year to allow the club and the player 'an opportunity of adjusting their affairs'. It was also stressed that this was a preliminary finding and the Committee would be giving further consideration to the case. A letter to that effect was duly sent on 4 November 1958.

The Northamptonshire reply was long and suitably pained. It pointed out that the agreement in question had been negotiated in August 1957 – in other words, before Duke Bernard's Committee had been constituted – in good faith and in accordance with the circumstances of the time. It was 'unfair and unjustifiable' to impose conditions which did not obtain at the time of the original agreement. Furthermore, in a sideswipe at Duke Bernard's Committee, it condemned as 'quite illogical' that compensation for loss of earnings should be paid on tour and not domestically. Finally, since Subba Row was at the time touring Australia with the MCC (and, of course, receiving 'broken time' payments as agreed by the Special Committee) the matter should be held over until he returned.

This letter was duly considered by the Standing Committee at their meeting of 8 December. The result was a terse reply to Northamptonshire to the effect that the Committee was governed by its terms of reference, which were quite explicit in the matter. Moreover, they believed that accepted practice 'by long custom' had been that such compensation was not paid to an amateur. They agreed, however, that the matter could be held in abeyance until Subba Row's return. Finally, they held out an olive branch by saying that the 'period of leniency' had been extended by decision of the Advisory County Cricket Committee and that no decision of the Standing Committee would take effect before 1 April 1960.

In the end, Northamptonshire felt obliged to give way. After discussions with Subba Row on his return from Australia, and with the imminent arrival of the date in 1960 when the axe would fall, they wrote to Aird with the news that the agreement with Subba Row had been terminated by mutual consent. The player himself, however, had indicated that he did not wish to become a professional and that therefore he would be unable to continue playing first-class cricket after the end of the 1960 season. He did in fact play one more season before retiring, at the age of twenty-nine, to seek a new career. For the record, he had played for England thirteen times, had made more than 14,000 runs in first-class cricket at an average of 41.46 and had scored no less than 300 against Surrey at the Oval in 1958, batting for nine hours and twenty-six minutes. In short, the 'Star Chamber' had claimed its first – illustrious – victim.

Donald Carr's was an easier case. But it had a special sensitivity given Carr's reputation and popularity at Derbyshire. In fact, he had come to Derbyshire after a peripatetic early life. Born in 1926 in Germany into a military family – his father was an officer in the Royal Berkshire Regiment who had played cricket and hockey for the Army before his retirement in 1936 to take up the post of Bursar at Repton public school – he took to sport in early youth and turned out to be something of a schoolboy wonder. Cricket was his preferred sport, both at preparatory school and then at Repton, although he was a natural athlete and took easily to football, hockey and squash. At the beginning of 1945 he joined the Army and, after a brief posting to Northern Ireland, went to Sandhurst. Even before he got there, however, he had been selected to play for an England side against the Australian Services in the third Victory Test – his debut in first-class cricket. Commissioned to the Royal Berkshire Regiment in February 1946, he played for Combined Services and Derbyshire during the summer but without great success. A posting to Burma took him out of cricket for 1947. Quite why he left the Army at that point is uncertain, but leave he did and then went up to Oxford University. The transition from matting wickets back to grass turned out not to be easy and it was not until his second year, 1949, that he won his Blue, went to play for Derbyshire and to make a total of 1,210 runs for the season. He toured India and Pakistan with the MCC in 1951–2 and played two Tests there, but thereafter was unable to challenge for a regular batting place among the England stars of the day and thereafter was confined to a county career with Derbyshire. He captained the county from 1955 to 1962, and by the end of his career had made over 10,000 runs for them.

As a batsman Carr was right-handed, athletic and particularly strong on the back foot, cutting and pulling with notable ferocity. On the front foot he would be happier playing to leg than to the off – he seemed permanently to lack an off drive – but he was a quick runner between the wickets. As a bowler he was initially a left-arm orthodox finger spinner but he changed, when at Oxford, to bowling wrist-spin off breaks (known as 'chinamen') and googlies, taking more than 300 first-class wickets in 450 matches. In his preferred position, as a close fielder, he was generally recognised to be one of the best in the country. As a captain he was respected and popular – although there were those who thought him rather too military in his approach and lacking the occasionally required relaxed and easy charm. (In later life, when he was in the forefront of cricket administration, he seems to have mellowed. In his smoother middle age he was almost universally popular with his colleagues.)

On leaving Oxford, Carr had taken a job with a Midlands brewery but he soon was offered, and accepted, the job of Assistant Secretary to Derbyshire County Cricket Club for which he was paid £850 annually. The proviso, of course, was that he would be released to play for the county as and when required. It seemed to be a clear example of 'shamateurism'. But on investigation it turned out that not only were Carr's secretarial duties genuine but that he was being trained to take over as full-time Secretary on the retirement of the then incumbent. The Committee duly found this arrangement consistent with their remit and, with something of a collective sigh of relief, declared Carr's amateur status *bona fide*.

The third case was that of Peter Richardson of Worcestershire. In contrast to Subba Row and Carr, Richardson was not a public school product. His family were farmers, first just outside Hereford and subsequently near Worcester. There was no history of first-class cricket in the family – Richardson's father was a club cricketer – but all three sons, Peter, Dick and Brian (all left-handed, as it happens), played in the first-class game, although with varying degrees of success. Richardson himself was soon spotted by Worcester while still at school but it took some time for him to mature sufficiently, both in technique and character, for selection to the county side. In fact, 1952 was his first decisive year: he was picked to open the batting with the old stalwart Don Kenyon and did so well that he scored more than 1,500 runs in the season and was duly awarded his county cap. He was equally successful in his first full season with England, with 81 and 73 in the first Ashes Test of 1956, a further 104 in 'Laker's Test' at Old Trafford and 491 Test runs for the whole season. As a result he was first-choice opening bat for England in the 1957 series against the West Indies and the 1958 series against New Zealand. But he had an unhappy Ashes tour of 1958–9, was out of cricket for a year while he qualified for his new county, Kent, and lost his Test place. Thereafter, apart from a tour of India and Pakistan and a 1963 Test against the West Indies, he concentrated on playing for Kent until his retirement in 1965.

Richardson was an aggressive left-hand bat who believed, as he said himself, in 'taking the game to the bowler'. Like Subba Row, he was also a master of the quick single to keep his score moving. Like many left-handers, he was particularly fond of the square cut but he could drive as well on both sides of the wicket (but also, like many left-handers, had a propensity to be caught at the wicket or in the gully). Sharp in the field, he was a respected captain and a popular colleague. A supremely jovial character, he was given to playing pranks, to entertaining anyone who would listen with jokes, stories both true and untrue and wild, infectious laughter. All in all, he was a joy to be with.

When they came to consider Richardson's case, the Standing Committee noted that they had been advised that he was paid, as the Worcester County Cricket Club's Assistant Secretary, an annual salary of £850 following an agreement dated 1 April 1958. They had also been told – wrongly as it turned out – that Richardson had a contract of employment with the Dudley Iron and Steel Company to perform unspecified tasks in relation to sales of the company's products. After taking note of all this, the Committee formally invited the Chairman and Secretary of Worcestershire County Cricket Club to a meeting at Lord's to discuss the matter.

The meeting duly took place on 16 October 1958. Rait Kerr opened proceedings by emphasising the 'invidious' nature of the Committee's task and stressing that the Committee 'wished most earnestly' to be both fair and reasonable. That done, he asked for an assurance that the annual salary of £850 paid to Richardson was for administrative duties only. Shelmerdine followed up by stating that £850, taken together with what they assumed – without any evidence – to be a further £750 from the (non-existent) contract with the Dudley Iron and Steel Company, could give neither the club nor the company a proper return for their money if Richardson was always absent in the summer playing for the county and in the winter touring with the MCC. The exchange became ill-tempered when the Worcestershire Chairman claimed that Richardson's arrangement with the Dudley Iron and Steel Company, whatever it might be, was none of their business provided it did not interfere with the performance of his duties for the club. Furthermore, if Richardson left the club for any reason they would still need to employ a replacement at the same salary. The Standing Committee duly considered Rait Kerr's report of the meeting on 29 October. They were not satisfied, and Aird was instructed to draft a letter to Worcestershire to that effect. Nevertheless, judgement was suspended for the time being – at least until a subsequent contract with Richardson due to be signed in April 1959.

Peter Richardson turned professional soon afterwards. The 'Star Chamber' had apparently claimed another scalp. But by the late autumn of 1958 there were mutterings. On 7 November Aird wrote to Rait Kerr to say that some of the county clubs thought that the MCC was interfering too much in their domestic affairs and asking for information which they thought both unnecessary and private. The upshot was that the Standing Committee at its meeting of 8 December decided that it had done its work – at least for the moment – and could go into temporary recess. In doing so, they noted that there might be another 'special case', Reg Simpson of Nottinghamshire, who apparently had some sort of contract with his county club. But that, for the moment, could wait.

Rait Kerr duly reported to a meeting of Duke Bernard's Special Committee on 26 January 1959. At the outset, however, even before Rait Kerr could make his report, Duke Bernard made two announcements: first, since his year as MCC President had finished in October 1958 he had expected to be replaced as Chairman of the Special Committee by the incoming President, Viscount Portal of Hungerford, but Lord Portal had asked him to continue; secondly, somewhat to the astonishment of the assembled Committee members, he announced that he had changed his mind. Try as they might to retain it, he said, amateur status as they had understood it had in his view come to an end. Of course, they had hoped that the recommendations in their Report would work but, sadly, they had not. Now, he felt, was the time for reconsideration. Duke Bernard was then supported (as had obviously been planned) by Altham, who followed up by emphasising the problems facing the Standing Committee in carrying out its 'difficult and dangerous' task. This and other matters, he said, had persuaded him, along with Duke Bernard, that whatever decisions were taken amateur status could not be preserved.

Rait Kerr then gave his report to the startled members. The Standing Committee, he said, had encountered the problems Altham had referred to. There had been a good deal of uneasiness. The lives and livelihood of some players had been affected. There had been 'difficulties and unpleasantness'. The Standing Committee, he went on, had not wished to challenge the Special Committee's Report, but he had the impression that the county clubs no longer supported its findings. In short, he agreed with Duke Bernard that the time had come for reconsideration. Both Sellers and Hastilow intervened to support him, Hastilow believing that the dividing line was so fine that means of evading the regulations could and would be found. Insole, on the other hand, thought that if county clubs paid their 'amateurs' firms employing them would not be prepared to pay them as at present and might possibly be less inclined to release them to play cricket.

Insole had, almost inadvertently, put his finger on the main flaw in the MCC's position. If it was wrong for Subba Row to be employed by a county club essentially to play cricket as an amateur, why was it right for Subba Row to be employed by Noel Gay for the same purpose? Once that question was put, there were numerous other examples of amateurs being so employed by friendly companies on the same basis – for instance, a large section of the Northamptonshire side employed by British Timken, or Colin Ingleby-Mackenzie of Hampshire employed by Slazenger, Insole himself employed by Wimpey or many others. Indeed, Duke Bernard only had to look on his own doorstep to find that he was employing Robin Marlar of

Sussex as his archivist at Arundel Castle on terms which allowed him to play first-class cricket wherever and whenever he wished. Marlar was a fine bowler and an intelligent individual but he certainly was not a trained archivist (in fact, the Arundel archives have still not been fully catalogued to this day).

The result was that all of us amateurs of the day could be, and were, investigated by what Wilf Wooller called the 'Star Chamber' to see whether we were covertly receiving money, above legitimate expenses, from the counties for which we were playing and, if so, under what circumstances, while nobody asked us for the terms of any employment with firms which had no 'connection' with the county club (which, of course, they did in the form of membership privileges, contacts with players, tickets and invitations to receptions and so on). In truth, it had become plain not just to Aird but to the whole of the Standing Committee in their investigations into the Subba Row and Richardson cases that neither they nor the county clubs in question had any possible locus for asking either the players or the employers to reveal the terms of their contracts of employment. Nor could they delve into the question of who had been responsible for arranging the employment in the first place. Yet without that information – and in particular the relations between firms, however informal, and the clubs – there could be no proper determination of true amateur status.

It was Sussex County Cricket Club which launched the missile which in the end undermined the whole MCC position. They pointed out, as others had, the illogicality of allowing 'broken time' payments to amateurs for overseas tours but not for domestic matches. But they went further. By allowing amateurs to accept employment for the periods when they were not required to play cricket, and on the understanding that they would take leave of absence from their employment when required to appear for their counties or their country, their services could be properly ensured by them not being paid by their employers while they were on leave of absence and playing cricket but receiving 'broken time' payments from county clubs in lieu. This procedure, they argued, would give true, logically coherent and practical effect to the principal recommendation of the Special Committee Report that the object of the whole exercise was to keep the best amateur players in the game. The consequence would be that the threat of premature amateur retirements along the lines of the Subba Row case would thus be permanently lifted.

It was impossible to deny the logic of the Sussex position. Moreover, it was the more powerful in that the President of Sussex CCC was none other than Duke Bernard himself. The underlying argument, that he would not have to pay Marlar during the cricket season on the understanding that the player would be suitably recompensed by his county club, was certainly appealing. Furthermore, whatever else he was Duke Bernard was no hypocrite. He had been firm in his view, in the original enquiry, that 'broken time' at home was inconsistent with amateur status and once that opinion had been crystallised in the Special Committee's Report it could not be overturned. On the other hand, the Sussex logic was compelling and, coming as it did from his own county (and with direct relevance to one of his own employees), demanded serious attention. It is little wonder that Duke Bernard had come to the conclusion that the whole matter of amateur status needed to be reconsidered – in short, that he had changed his mind.

The meeting of 26 January 1959 then broke up in some confusion. The only agreement reached was to meet again soon for a further discussion. In the meantime the members of the Special Committee were invited to ponder the dilemma they faced. True to form, having thus pondered, they reconvened on 20 February. They were met with another piece of disturbing news. At the outset, Aird reported that Sussex CCC had copied their original submission to the Special Committee to members of the Advisory County Cricket Committee. There would probably be, he went on, a discussion at the next meeting of their committee the following month – although the agenda had already been set and there could be no decision on the matter. On hearing this news, Duke Bernard led a long and rather rambling discussion, going yet again over the familiar ground of amateur status. At the end of it, it was agreed that yet another memorandum should be drafted and, on Rait Kerr's suggestion, that the county clubs should be invited to send representatives to a joint meeting with the Special Committee itself.

The memorandum, when it came, was entitled, rather bleakly, 'Amateur Status Problem'. It began by rehearsing the reasons why the Special Committee thought it right 'to review the whole position again'. First, the question of 'broken time' payments had been raised again – and refused to go away. Secondly, the task of establishing a universal standard to decide whether a player should be considered to be amateur or professional had proved to be much more difficult than had been expected. It went on to explain the reasons for the original 1958 recommendations, to admit that there had been differences of opinion within the Committee and, in view of that divergence, to invite counties 'to give further consideration to the problem'. The memorandum was approved at a Special Committee meeting on 16 July and sent out to counties with an invitation to them to appoint one representative to come to a conference of Special Committee members on Monday 19 October 1959.

In all, some twenty-six people (all, of course, male, white and mostly middle-aged) turned up for what they regarded as a crucial conference. They were welcomed by Duke Bernard, who chaired the event. In welcoming representatives from first-class counties as well as his fellow members of the Special Committee he explained that no decisions would be taken but that the Special Committee hoped that the county representatives would fully state their views as a guide to their future deliberations.

They took full advantage of Duke Bernard's invitation. The contributions were extensive in length – although in most cases lacking in any new insight. 'Broken time' payment to amateurs in domestic games was, on the insistence of Sussex, given a full hearing. Allowances to amateur cricketers was next on the agenda, with most contributions leaning towards the view that counties should be left to do what they felt fit. As Tom Pearce of Essex pointed out, if professionals did not like the arrangement they could always turn amateur. Wilf Wooller stated, somewhat inconsequentially, that in the case of table tennis the terms 'amateur' and 'professional' were not used.

At the end of an exhausting morning, Duke Bernard concluded the conference. The final decision on all these matters, he reminded them, would rest with the MCC Committee on the recommendation of the Special Committee. Nevertheless, his Committee hoped, as a result of the meeting, to have a clear idea of the view of the county clubs. He therefore proposed to put some of the issues to a vote.

The count, when taken, went as follows:

1. The abolition of the distinction between amateurs and professionals.
   2 yes; 15 no

2. Payment of 'broken time' in England.
   5 yes; 12 no

3. Tightening up on the amateur.
   5 yes; 8 no; 4 abstentions

4. Maintaining the status quo as it existed before the special enquiry – in other words 'shutting a blind eye' (an odd expression but one which was used at the time).
   4 yes; 11 no; 2 abstentions

5. Maintaining the status quo with control in accordance with rules laid down by the Special Committee.
   12 yes; 3 no; 2 abstentions.

The Advisory County Cricket Committee duly met on 18 November to review the results of the conference. The Chairman, the new MCC President Harry Altham, felt that it had been an interesting 'if at times baffling' discussion in which most of those present had felt that they were 'groping for a solution to a well-nigh impossible problem'. As he reported, 'the only proposition which was carried was that in favour of maintaining the status of the amateur'. Beyond that, he said, 'the buck had been passed firmly back to the Special Committee'. The results of their deliberations would, he proposed, be reviewed at their next meeting in March 1960.

In his letter of 4 December to all members of the Special Committee summoning them to a meeting on 18 January 1960 to discuss the results of the conference and the conclusion of the November meeting of the Advisory County Cricket Committee, Aird reported the conclusions faithfully. But in doing so he cleverly finessed the question of what should now be done. He maintained that the only matter which had not been closed at the conference was that of the level of amateurs' expenses. It followed that the main focus of the Special Committee's attention should be on that. He therefore invited – and received – submissions from county clubs on their current practice.

Aird, as a good official, had tried to seal off potential damage to the Committee of which he was a servant. But he was not wholly successful. As the caravan moved onward into 1960 the Amateur Status Standing Committee was again called into action. At the January meeting of the Special Committee, after a 'long discussion', it had agreed (quite erroneously and apparently without any degree of shame) that the county representatives had 'clearly expressed their approval of the original

Report' and that 'it was now up to the Special Committee to put the Report into operation'.

What this meant in practice was that county clubs received yet another request – this time from the Standing Committee (although the writing paper was always MCC standard) – to provide a list, similar to that of 1958, of amateurs on their registered list for 1960 who received emoluments either from the club itself or from any organisation associated with the club. Furthermore, there were three doubtful cases carried over from 1958 which needed to be resolved. It turned out that Richardson had turned professional, Simpson no longer had a contract with Nottinghamshire and Subba Row was in the process of negotiating his way out of his agreement with Northamptonshire. That done, however, other cases might turn up and it was therefore necessary to repeat the 1958 procedure.

In the event, the Standing Committee was able to report, at its meeting of 19 July 1960, that all cases had been cleared up and that no further action need be taken. Moreover, on Rait Kerr's proposal, it was agreed that it should only be necessary to hold one meeting a year in order to make a review of registered players – and that this meeting should be held in April. A new pro forma should be introduced for each player whose amateur status was being considered and returned to the MCC with the county's annual list of registered players.

By the end of the 1960 season it seemed that the ultimate prize had finally been won – a settled form of amateur status which would survive the turbulence of the times. But it was not long – in fact the following year

– before that particular dawn was shown to be false. In another fit of bad temper Wilf Wooller derided the whole state of affairs as 'ridiculous' and claimed that the system would before long be overturned. Aird's efforts to keep the show, as it were, creakily on the road were in the end to come to nothing.

9

THE FINAL DECLARATION

'I have always thought the Amateur Status Standing Committee a stupid idea but I am now quite certain that it is stark raving mad'

By the end of the 1960 English cricket season there had been something of a shift of influence away from the MCC Committee and Duke Bernard's Special Committee towards the county clubs and what was in truth their own committee (admittedly under MCC auspices) the ACCC. It was, after all, the county clubs which were ultimately responsible for the practicalities of the domestic first-class game. But the shift did not make for greater coherence. In fact, it made for just the opposite, since at its meeting on 16 November 1960 the ACCC decided to invite the MCC to set up yet another committee, to enquire, 'with particular reference to the financial situation of the County Clubs', into the state of first-class cricket and consider whether any changes 'in its structure and/or in the general conduct of the game' were needed. The committee was to be given the name 'Cricket Enquiry Committee' and was to report directly not to the MCC Committee but to the ACCC.

The incoherence became more apparent when the

membership of the Cricket Enquiry Committee was (very discreetly) released. In fact, it drew heavily on the membership of Duke Bernard's Special Committee. Aird, Allen, Hastilow, Insole, Sellers, Sheppard, Howard, May and Wooller were all there. The wheel seemed to have turned full circle. The missing figure, of course, was Duke Bernard himself, as the Committee was presided over by the then President, Sir Hubert Ashton. But the transition from the Duke to the knight was seamless. Ashton was made from the same mould (and, for that matter, the same mould that had produced the previous Presidents Lords Monckton and Portal). In short, he was a true gentleman – courteous, patriotic, religious, well-spoken – and irredeemably conservative. Like his contemporaries he had fought in the First World War (and won the Military Cross), had played his cricket in the years after the war for Cambridge and, as was proper for an amateur, Essex in the vacations. He joined Burmah Oil Ltd in 1922 and, while posted to India, played – perhaps surprisingly – for India in a match against an MCC touring side in 1926–7 and playing again for Essex later in the summer of 1927. After the Second World War, Ashton went into politics and was elected Conservative MP for Chelmsford in 1950. The job was coupled not with any ministerial preferment but with the Presidency of Essex County Cricket Club, with a knighthood in 1959 and the Presidency of the MCC for 1960–61. A kindly man – although perhaps rather dull – with few harsh words even for his wildest political opponents (including C. C. P. Williams who became Labour candidate for Colchester in 1961), he was not expected to sponsor radical changes to the established cricket format.

Setting up the Cricket Enquiry Committee led to some unexpected consequences. Ken Turner, for instance, the Northamptonshire Secretary, wrote formally on 15 February 1961 to hope that the Amateur Status Standing Committee and the MCC would now 'postpone this issue of amateurism' (in other words the Subba Row affair) until 'we know at least what shape cricket is going to take in the future'. Since the Cricket Enquiry Committee was to avoid the 'issue of amateurism' at its first meeting on 21 February this turned out to be a forlorn hope. It provoked a terse reply from Aird to Turner saying that the Amateur Status Standing Committee was governed by the conclusions of Duke Bernard's Special Committee and that, as it were, was that.

Worse, however, was to come when one of the biggest guns in the army of cricket administrators, Wilf Wooller fired off another series of intemperate salvoes. On 16 March 1961 he wrote to Aird that 'the "Star Chamber" should be advised' that Glamorgan County Cricket Club had engaged the former Cambridge Blue O. S. Wheatley as Public Relations Officer at a salary of £650 per annum. It was proposed to meet his salary by using his efforts to recruit a further 2,500 supporters to the supporters' club. In addition, however, 'he will have quite an amount of cricket duties'. This last assertion was perhaps disingenuous. Wooller's plan was to pass the captaincy of the county to Wheatley when the time came for him to retire. (This was not a bad idea. 'Ossie' Wheatley was a cheerful enough character – something of a contrast to Wooller – and a more than competent fast-medium left-arm seam bowler.)

There was then a good deal of to and fro. On request, Wooller was more specific. Wheatley was employed by Welsh Television (TWW) and in order for him to become better known in Wales he would be allowed time off to play cricket full time during the season for two years. Moreover, TWW had agreed that during those two years Glamorgan County Cricket Club should have a part-time claim on his public relations services. Finally, the club was well off and could easily afford Wheatley's salary. 'I trust this explains the situation fully,' Wooller concluded in his letter of 23 March. 'And I may say', he added, 'it causes me intense irritation to have to do it. I think this whole idea quite one of the stupidest that has been introduced since the War.'

It was not a helpful continuation of what was supposed to be a dialogue. Aird, restraining his temper, duly consulted the Amateur Status Standing Committee. Their verdict was unanimous, and on 11 April he replied to Wooller that O. S. Wheatley could not accept the payment of £650 and remain an amateur. Furthermore, since Wheatley was the subject of an application for Special Registration to be allowed to play for Glamorgan it would be necessary to make the MCC's Registration Committee aware of the arrangement.

There was then a further explosion from Cardiff. 'I have always thought', Wooller replied the following day, 'the Amateur Status Standing Committee a stupid idea but I am now quite certain that it is stark raving mad.' Wheatley was already working for TWW. Part of his job with Glamorgan would be to increase the membership of both the club itself and the supporters' club. He would thus pay for himself. As a professional he would cost the club £900 a year for cricket and a further £400–£500 for outside services, an idea which was quite 'scatter-brained'. Wooller then threatened to resign from all MCC Committees and Sub-Committees and to make his objections public. 'No Committee I know', he concluded, 'has brought such ridicule to the game when it least can afford it and when it contains such glaring anomolies [*sic*] as the undercover payments to certain players, to say little of the sums earned by Trevor Bailey, Peter May etc. for advertising, writing etc. … it just does not make sense.'

Aird's formal reply was precise and to the point. He had spoken to all members of the Amateur Status Standing Committee, and he wrote on 14 April (in measured tones) to assure Wooller that there would be no objection to Wheatley being paid by results, for example by a commission on the receipts to the club as a result of his work (always assuming that the commission rates were the same as those for others doing the same job). A note of irritation then crept in. 'You mention undercover payments made to certain players. The Amateur Status Standing Committee have no knowledge of any such payments. The Standing Committee are doing their best to carry out a very difficult and thankless job on behalf of the Counties. Their task is an impossible one if the Counties do not show loyalty and co-operation.'

But in a private letter to Wooller of the same date Aird was much more forthright. His patience had quite clearly snapped. 'Dear Wilfred', the letter runs, 'You have written a good many pretty offensive letters to me in the past and yours of April 12th is yet another. I do not mind what

sort of letters you write to me personally but I think it is
time you stopped writing these [*sic*] sort of letters to me
as Secretary of MCC ... No other County Secretary has
ever written to me in the terms that you so often do, and
I hope that you will discontinue this practice ... rude and
offensive letters do no good to anyone ... the suggestion
in the fourth paragraph of your letter of April 12th about
resigning from Sub-Committees and reserving the right
to make your views known publicly is the statement of a
"small man", which you are not ... I have always valued
your friendship and would like it to continue, so please do
not make it difficult for me by writing any more offensive
letters.'

Wooller just managed to apologise to Aird for his rude-
ness but certainly was not going back on his objections
to the Amateur Status Standing Committee, the forma-
tion of which, as he claimed in his next missive, he had
opposed from the start. He went on to assert: 'I know for
a fact that a number of Secretaries are worried about it
and in my opinion it is preventing a number of amateurs
coming into the game ... by heavens we need them ...
why in heavens name [devise] a set up that had it oper-
ated over the last 50 years would have excluded some of
the greatest players in the game?' Nevertheless, he did
agree to put Wheatley on commission rather than salary.
The outcome was duly reported to the members of the
Amateur Status Standing Committee who agreed that the
case had been settled satisfactorily.

Leaving aside the bad temper involved, Wooller had
made his point. Hastilow believed that the solution
was to invite the ACCC to reopen the whole issue of

amateur status. Aird, however, thought that the right course of action was to wait for the report of the Cricket Enquiry Committee. Unfortunately, the Chairman of that Committee, Rait Kerr, had died early in April and the Committee had decided not to hold any more meetings before the autumn. The stalemate was thus complete – at least until the end of the English cricket season of 1961.

It was 23 November before the Committee, now under Ashton's chairmanship, met again. They considered a report of a sub-committee which had been set up to study the structure of the first-class game and the text of their own interim report of which the sub-committee's report would form the Appendix. A one-day knockout competition, in addition to the championship, was proposed. It was noted that attendances at three-day games was still slipping (1961 attendances at just under one million for the season against nearly two million for 1951 were the lowest recorded since the Second World War) and the overall financial deficit, even after taking into account all receipts other than gate money, amounted to an average of £120,000 per annum over the five years 1956–60. Some form of remedial action was called for and a knockout competition seemed as good an idea as any.

This recommendation was presented to a special meeting of the ACCC on 20 December 1961. By a vote of 10 to 8 the introduction of a knockout competition was rejected for 1962 but, by 14 votes to 3, it was accepted for 1963. Unfortunately, what nobody at the meeting had noticed was that such a competition would affect the status of the amateur. During a season in which the county championship was settled not on a knockout basis but over the whole summer it was possible for counties to accept that amateurs could, provided they were good enough, come and go as they pleased. Such an arrangement was impossible in a knockout competition when counties would wish to field their strongest sides and therefore demand the presence of their best players – be they amateur or professional.

This problem started to dawn on the Cricket Enquiry Committee at its meeting on 8 February 1962. Although the discussion took place around the possibility of payments to amateurs (everybody was against 'broken time'), the general feeling developed, reflecting Duke Bernard's own feeling of two years earlier, that the whole system was unsatisfactory – and would become more so after the ACCC decision to start a knockout competition in 1963. A resolution that 'broken time' should not be paid in England was carried without dissent but somewhat to their own surprise the Committee then carried 'by a substantial majority' a resolution, proposed by Sellers and seconded by Alec Bedser, 'that the ACCC be asked to re-open the whole question of amateur status with a view to considering the desirability of classifying all first class players as cricketers instead of being called amateurs and professionals as heretofore'. The language of the resolution may have been tortuous but the intention was plain.

Although Ashton remained Chairman of the Cricket Enquiry Committee the Presidency of the MCC itself had passed in October 1961 to Colonel Sir William Arthur Worsley of Hovingham, then President of Yorkshire CCC and Lord Lieutenant of the North Riding of Yorkshire

– and father of the new Duchess of Kent. Worsley was, by any standards, a chip from the same block as Duke Bernard, the Lords Monckton and Portal and Sir Hubert Ashton (perhaps he ranked socially a notch above Ashton but the distinction was fine). He had served, like them, in the First World War, had been wounded and taken prisoner, played a modest part as captain of Yorkshire in 1928 and 1929 – scoring 733 runs at an average of 16.28 – and drifted effortlessly into highest position in the MCC.

Worsley, like his predecessors, was a gentle soul but he was no radical. Nor was he a conspicuously good Chairman. To be sure, the meeting of the ACCC of 14 March 1962 at which he was to preside to consider the request of the Cricket Enquiry Committee on amateur status was, as usual, unwieldy (there was an attendance of no fewer than forty-one) and had a long agenda, but Worsley did not seem to appreciate, in agreeing the agenda, that the request was a matter of the highest importance and should therefore be taken as first or second item – certainly before many members' concentration would be deflected by thoughts of lunch. But when it came to it they ploughed laboriously through the minutes, matters arising, arrangements for the Pakistan tour that summer (they were told that the headquarters of the Pakistan team would be Berners Hotel), preliminary arrangements for the West Indies tour of 1963, appeals against the light in county matches and a long wrangle about the rules of registration.

It was only after all that business that the ACCC got round to considering the submission of the Cricket Enquiry Committee. First they dealt with the distribution of television fees. Only after that did they come to the proposal on amateur status. Worsley, on Aird's advice, told them that they could not hold a vote on the matter since there was no firm proposition before them. Aird then recounted the history of the controversy, by which time they were all both tired and hungry. There was a short discussion after which it was unanimously agreed that 'the Cricket Enquiry Committee should produce a memorandum on the subject and make a recommendation to the ACCC at its meeting in November'. With that, after a desultory discussion of a few other items and a vote of thanks to Worsley for his conduct of the meeting, the members drifted off to a most welcome lunch.

The Cricket Enquiry Committee, when they met on 25 April, were rather taken aback by the ACCC resolution. Their Chairman – still Hubert Ashton, although Worsley was present *ex officio* at the meeting – wondered out loud whether such an undertaking was strictly within their terms of reference and jurisdiction. He was firmly reassured by the Treasurer, Harry Altham, but pointed out that he was not prepared to take a vote on the matter and would confine the discussion to expression of opinions which might guide a sub-committee when it was set up. There followed another rambling debate which revealed little that had not been said before, although it was noted that those previously in strong support of amateur status were more muted – not least Aird himself. At the end of the debate it was agreed to set up a sub-committee to produce a memorandum on the matter for their next meeting at the end of May. Significantly, however, the membership of three was heavily slanted towards abolition:

Ashton himself, who was neutral, Alec Bedser and David Sheppard, who were both abolitionists.

The memorandum was largely drafted by Jim Dunbar, given the task in his capacity as Assistant Secretary of the MCC. As such, it has a fairly ponderous tone. In the section entitled 'Background' it rehearsed the history of Duke Bernard's Special Committee and the subsequent developments in the matter. It noted, in passing, that nine members of Duke Bernard's Committee were now members of the Cricket Enquiry Committee discussing the same subject nearly five years later. It then went on to describe the familiar themes which had been aired, yet again, at the meeting of 25 April and suggested that the 'problem' could 'probably be resolved by taking one of three courses'.

The first course was described as 'A': 'to retain the status quo of the amateur and to continue applying the rules as laid down in the [1958] Report of the Special Committee'. The second course was 'B': 'to review the present definition of an amateur and impose such restrictions as would comply with the definition of a genuine amateur who receives only his out of pocket expenses for playing cricket'. The third course was 'C': 'to abolish the restriction between the amateur and the professional and to regard all players as cricketers'. There followed a summary of the views expressed to the Sub-Committee (it would be tedious to recite them all since all were only too well known). With that, the memorandum was presented to the Cricket Enquiry Committee for discussion and decision at its meeting of 29 May 1962.

The meeting duly took place at Lord's in the afternoon

of 29 May. Nineteen members were present and there were apologies from five others. Sir Hubert Ashton was in the chair. He went round the table to canvass the views of all members. As he did so it seemed that the difficulties of maintaining amateur status as at present understood were weighing heavily with members, particularly those who had responsibility for their county clubs. In the end, John Warr of Middlesex, supported by Hastilow, proposed that 'C' (abolition of restriction between amateurs and professionals) should be passed and recommended to the ACCC. An amendment to his proposal was put by Aird, supported by Gubby Allen that 'A' rather than 'C' should be recommended (maintaining amateur status as at present) but disallowing amateurs from participating in advertisements or putting their names on cricket equipment. When put to the vote, Aird's amendment was carried by seven votes to six with six abstentions. A letter was duly drafted and sent on 27 June 1962 to the ACCC enclosing the memorandum and recommending that proposal 'C' be adopted.

Before the next ACCC meeting, scheduled for November 1962, there were some important interventions. Wooller again came to the fore, and in writing to Aird on 14 September was more than usually colourful. 'There has been much talk', he wrote, 'full of sound and fury but it has signified little ... while the tentacles of our massive inactivity are slowly strangling us all, would it not be wisdom to sever the odd one and show some signs of legislative life to the watching populace? They might in due course think that our life was worth saving and come to our rescue.' On behalf of Glamorgan CCC he proposed the abolition of the amateur/professional distinction. He was supported by Sussex but opposed by Kent which wished to retain the status quo. Gubby Allen and Maurice Allom wrote a memorandum for the MCC Committee itself urging caution – and the appointment of another committee on the matter.

The stage was thus set for the meeting of the ACCC held at Lord's on the morning of Monday 26 November. The incoming MCC President, Lord Nugent, was in the chair and some forty-three representatives of the counties were present. After a presentation to Ronnie Aird who was retiring as Secretary (the minutes record that he was going to use his parting gift to furnish his new house in Sandwich) the meeting got down to business. In all it took, with one break for lunch, no less than six hours.

The first substantive item on the agenda was the question of amateur status. Ashton, as Chairman of the Cricket Enquiry Committee, led the debate. He explained the background to the Cricket Enquiry Committee's recommendation and formally moved it. He was supported by Tom Pearce of Essex. Wilf Wooller then set out his counter proposal – abolition. He in turn was supported by A. K. Wilson of Sussex. Eagar, for Hampshire, was in full support of Ashton and the Cricket Enquiry Committee. He in turn was supported by Allom for Surrey (who wanted amateurs to be allowed to advertise and sign bats), J. D. Eggar for Derbyshire and D. G. Clark of Kent. A. C. Payne of Derbyshire, Reg Simpson for Nottinghamshire and Sellers for Yorkshire spoke in favour of Wooller and Sussex. On being asked the MCC view, Harry Altham, the MCC Treasurer, hedged. It was, he said, one of the most important issues ever to come before the ACCC but before any final decision was taken on amateur status a 'sub-committee should look into the possibilities of a change in structure'.

It was time for a vote (before lunch). Allom's amendment was defeated by 10 votes to 4 (each county had one vote only). A compromise proposal from Kent was defeated by 14 votes to 3. A similar majority defeated the recommendation of the Cricket Enquiry Committee. Finally, Wooller moved the Glamorgan proposal, seconded by Sussex. It was carried by 12 votes to 7. The deed was done.

The press were taken completely by surprise – as were Duke Bernard and Ted Dexter, then touring Australia. True, the cricket correspondent of *The Times* had noted the possibility that the amateurs' days might be over when he learnt that the Cricket Enquiry Committee had reopened the whole issue but their decision seemed to have put it back where it was. The ACCC reversal of that decision had come when the most influential journalists were with Duke Bernard's team following the Ashes Test series. As a consequence there were some hastily composed pieces despatched from Brisbane to Fleet Street. Most of them, in fact, carried the same message. The *Daily Mail*, for instance, applauded the death of 'humbug and the need for petty deception, a blot on cricket for years' while the *Daily Telegraph* simply noted that amateurs were making so much money from writing and advertising that a 'form of legalised deceit was being practised'. There were, of course, one or two dissenting voices – Jim Swanton lamented the passing of an era and the editor of *Wisden* was not altogether happy – but the general response was that the time had come to recognise that there were very few genuine amateurs in the first-class game and that the distinction between amateur and professional was so fine as to be at times undetectable.

The last step in the process was the agreement of the full MCC Committee. The majority in the ACCC had been 'clear but not overwhelming' and there was some doubt whether the MCC might hold it up. In the event, however, the decision was accepted at the Committee meeting of 31 January 1963 without dissent. The only practical problem which remained was to find a substitute fixture to replace the Gentlemen vs Players matches at Lord's and Scarborough. Apart from that, few seemed to realise, in the shock of the decision, that a whole era of cricket history had come to an abrupt end.

10

GENTLEMEN VS PLAYERS

'Cricket, lovely cricket ...'

In its early years the Gentlemen vs Players match at Lord's was notable for its anomalies. For a start, the 'Gentlemen' were often forced to rely on professionals to make up their side. In the first game, for instance, at Lord's in 1806, 'Silver Billy' Beldham and Bill Lambert, both professional stars from Hambledon, secured a resounding victory for the Gentlemen. Then the number of players on each side were varied according to circumstance (in 1836 the Gentlemen fielded eighteen against the Players' eleven – and still lost). There was also the problem of renting Thomas Lord's ground ahead of the pigeon shooting and hopping contests. Finally, it was always possible to vary the rules. In the so-called 'Barn Door' match of 1837, to give another instance, the Players were required to defend a wicket much larger than was customary (the stumps were one foot wide and three feet tall) – but they still won by an innings.

It was, it need hardly be said, all part of an effort to make the fixture attractive to the punters. They had lost interest in the early years since there was little point in backing the Gentlemen against the dominant Players. In fact, the fixture only survived in the middle years of the nineteenth century because the Gentlemen were prepared themselves to put up money to keep it going. The Players, for their part, were anxious to stop what had become something of a farce but money was, after all, money – and six shillings for a match was not at all to be sniffed at.

The fixture turned around with the arrival of the Grace brothers in the 1860s. The MCC decided to make them members and thus secure their amateur status – and qualification to play for the Gentlemen. It was a shrewd move. Such were their abilities, with both bat and ball, and their determination to perform well in the matches (by fair means or by means which fell short of fair), and such was the popular drawing power of W. G. that the fixture became firmly placed in the calendar and started to make a profit. Moreover, in the later years of the nineteenth century, the Grace era, the Gentlemen were able to hold their own against the Players and so give the punters some profitable sport.

After the First World War the fixture was resumed, not with great enthusiasm but as part of the 'return to normalcy'. There was an uninteresting drawn match in early July 1919 at the Oval (J. B. Hobbs made 120 not out), followed by another almost immediately afterwards at Lord's (J. B. Hobbs made a further 113). The Scarborough Festival took up the running in 1920 and by the mid-twenties there were regular matches at the Oval, Lord's and Scarborough, but the Oval dropped out soon after, leaving Lord's and Scarborough sharing the fixture.

The two fixtures, however, were quite different in character. The Lord's game, particularly in the 1930s when the results were evenly balanced, was at times fiercely competitive between the two sides. Scarborough, on the other hand, was played in something of a festive manner. On the eve of the game the Gentlemen, who were all invited to stay at the Grand Hotel, were treated to a sumptuous black-tie dinner by the President of the Festival in the hotel's Cricketers Room. The Players, who were not invited to the dinner, had to make do – unless they paid to stay at the Grand – with staying at the less smart Balmoral Hotel (nicknamed the 'Immoral' for obvious reasons) and were left to find their own sustenance. The result was that the Gentlemen tended to turn up the following morning much the worse for wear. Their mood was not helped by the presence of a brass band which played fortissimo throughout the day. There was some solace during the tea interval when footmen or waitresses would bring out a table and tablecloth, place them just off the square and proceed to serve the jaded cricketers with tea and cucumber sandwiches. (In fact, these lavish arrangements continued even after the Second World War, which may explain the lamentable performance of C. C. P. Williams in 1956.)

In the 1950s there was a sense of irreverence about the historic fixture. Simply told, it just did not seem right for the times. Attendances fell from the halcyon postwar days of over 20,000 at Lord's; amateurs felt able to decline the invitation to play; the atmosphere became more waspish (in 1958 the captain of the Players, Godfrey Evans, announced to his team: 'Gentlemen, it is time for the players to take the field' and, when Subba Row came in to bat, after a few overs told him: 'Before you came in I knew you were no Gentleman; now that I have seen you batting a bit I realize that you are not a Player either.').

By the time of the last Gentlemen vs Players matches, in 1962, it was apparent that both Lord's and Scarborough had become anachronisms. This was old-fashioned cricket, far removed from the enthusiasm of the West Indies calypso of 1951, 'cricket, lovely cricket ... '. Fortunately, the match at Lord's coincided with the meeting of the MCC Committee (who still held the responsibility of appointing the captain while the selectors appointed the side) who were to determine during the game who would captain the MCC side to tour Australasia the following winter. The full side was to be selected ten days later. This added spice to what otherwise would have been an unremarkable cricket game – and, incidentally, enlarged the attendance figures.

The three contenders for the captaincy were Cowdrey, Sheppard and Dexter. All three had their pluses and their minuses. Cowdrey had originally been appointed to captain the Gentlemen but had to withdraw to undergo an 'exploratory operation' for kidney stones. His abilities as a batsman and slip fielder, as well as his experience, were unquestioned but his health could be a problem and he was not seen as a strong personality. Sheppard was undoubtedly strong but he had been out of top-flight cricket for some time while training for the priesthood and there was doubt whether he could reach the required standard and at the same time captain an Ashes tour. Dexter's problem was one of inexperience – and what some perceived to be over-ebullience.

The match began on Wednesday 18 July. The weather was bright but rather windy, and the pitch was firm without looking too green. Dexter, standing in for Cowdrey as captain of the Gentlemen, won the toss and decided to bat. After losing an early wicket to Trueman, he came in himself to join Sheppard. The contrast between the two was apparent. Sheppard was playing cautiously, particularly against the medium pace of Shackleton and the off spin of Fred Titmus. Dexter, on the other hand, drove his second ball from Shackleton straight past the bowler for four – and continued in the same vein, standing a yard outside his crease to the faster bowlers and once hitting Shackleton back over his head. By lunch the Gentlemen were 101 for 1 wicket.

After lunch Dexter was soon out – for 55 – hitting too early at Shackleton's slower ball and being caught two-handed over his head by Trueman at deep mid off. Mike Smith took over to add another 95 with Sheppard who by then was showing his true form. Smith was eventually run out for 44 trying to steal a second run from Graveney fielding at deep square leg. After that, when Sheppard was out – after batting for four hours – caught and bowled by Titmus, the batting collapsed until some sturdy resistance from the tail took the total to 323 by the end of the day. Yet the press were satisfied that both Sheppard and Dexter had passed their respective tests.

By the next day the weather had changed. It was overcast with an occasional drizzle – weather to favour a seam bowler. Before very long the Players were 104 for 6 wickets, Trevor Bailey taking three of them, his first success coming off the fourth ball of the day. 'It must be a long time', *The Times* commented, 'since he bowled better than this', going on to note that he had certainly improved his chances of going to Australia. Wickets fell steadily until Titmus – guarding 'his wicket with arms and legs and pads and body like a policeman holding back a crowd' – and Trueman – with his 'bludgeon' – pulled the innings round to reach a total of 260. The Gentlemen were left a short time to bat at the end of the second day.

The highlight of the day, however, had been the announcement, soon after the tea interval, that Dexter had been nominated as captain for the 1962–3 Ashes tour. Sheppard, for his part, took the news well, promising full support (Cowdrey was undergoing surgery at Guy's Hospital at the time) and Dexter made a good fist of his press conference, promising suitably to take the game to Australia and believing that he would have players in his side with the resources to regain the Ashes. With that, he returned to what was still a gloomy day on the cricket field.

The third day of the match was something of an anti-climax after the excitement of the England captaincy appointment. R. M. Prideaux made a fine hundred, Dexter was cheered all the way to the wicket by the large crowd as well as the Players in the field – only to be run out almost immediately as the result of a muddle. As the cricket went on, early in the afternoon Dexter declared, to leave the Players to make 236 runs in just over three hours. They almost achieved this thanks to John Edrich and Peter Parfitt, but with thirty-five minutes left to play and only twenty-nine runs needed a rainstorm intervened and the game went to a soggy and unsatisfactory draw.

If the Lord's match ended with a wet whimper the Scarborough match in September was conducted in festive jocularity. The Gentlemen, batting first, were down to 189 for 8 before two tail-enders, G. W. Richardson and R. I. Jefferson, slogged a further 130 runs, treating Trueman, Lock and Barrington as though they were intruders into a game of village cricket. In response, the Players just overtook the Gentlemen's total of 328 thanks to a century from Barrington. In their second innings the Gentlemen did less well, bowled out for 217, which the Players knocked off for the loss of only three wickets. Suitably enough, the match also ended in the rain.

It was not a dignified ending to what had been, in its day, a fixture which had attracted much popular support. Yet the truth is that although nominally the Gentlemen were amateurs and the Players professionals there was by then little difference between the two. The officer class of the amateurs had disappeared and the other ranks had taken over. Dinners at the Grand in Scarborough were only an uneasy shadow of what they had been and the footmen no longer served tea on the field. All in all, it was time to fold whatever tents were left and move on to the professional game. There were few regrets. In the words of one participant, Walter Robins's son Charlie, the whole thing had become 'a bit of an embarrassment'.

THE WALK FROM THE PARKS

Eheu fugaces, Postume, Postume, labuntur anni

There is a simple bench, on the boundary of the cricket ground in the Oxford Parks, dedicated to the memory of Colin Cowdrey. It was placed there soon after his death in 2000, the cost of the bench and the inscription having been funded by those of us who had shared with Cowdrey the joy of his batting genius when he was at Oxford. There was no need for superlatives. It was enough to refer to him, as we did, simply as 'The Master'.

Not very long ago I went back to the Parks and sat for a time on the Cowdrey memorial bench. After reliving nostalgically the golden summers of the early 1950s, I decided to retrace the path that I had taken on the day my father died in 1943. As I walked on it seemed that nothing much had changed. The cricket pavilion in the Parks was just as shabby as before. Rhodes House stood – forbiddingly – where it had always stood. The Bodleian, to be sure, had been enhanced with a new building, but the way across the Broad, along the Turl, over the High and down to Canterbury Gate into Christ Church was what I had always known. It was easy to believe not that nothing much had changed but that nothing at all had changed.

Yet as I walked I reflected that below the surface much had indeed changed. In 1943 wartime Oxford had been a threadbare institution, its academic heart quiescent in the need to supply its pupils to the fighting of wars. Post-war Christ Church made a brave attempt to relive the excesses of *Brideshead Revisited* (the Bullingdon was in action again) but never quite succeeded. In fact, 'Austerity Britain', as it has been called (although it was also an age of hope) had brought with it not just economic hardship but an expansion of the whole educational system. By the early 1950s the composition of the student population was starting to change, not just in quantity but in social background. Christ Church might try to remain what it had been but Wadham and Keble – just two examples – welcomed the newcomers.

Yet change was slow. Britain was paying what Jean Monnet was to call 'the price of victory'. It was not just virtual bankruptcy – almost all European countries had that in common. The victors felt that in their triumph they could remain within the boundaries of their own past and change themselves within those boundaries – and with the same rows. Countries that had suffered defeat in the war felt bound to change from their pre-war structures, which in many cases had led directly to their subsequent collapse. As a result, new constitutions were drafted, new institutions created and new relationships formed. Most important of all were the efforts to ensure that a European war of such dimensions should never recur. The Council of Europe in 1948, a loose arrangement of sovereign countries, was a start. But a more ambitious project, the European Coal and Steel Community of 1951, involved at least partial surrender of national sovereignty to an international body.

Britain, having been on the winning side in the war, felt no need of a new constitution or new institutions, and would only participate in the Council of Europe – shying away from the Coal and Steel Community. The price of victory was the conviction, mistaken as it turned out, that we could satisfactorily look to our own affairs rather than embrace a vision which seemed only to be promoted by our defeated neighbours. In short, amid all the turbulence of the immediate post-war years there was an underlying desire to return to what was, in insular terms, familiar. As might be imagined, this was particularly true of the political right in society generally; and it need hardly be said that both the public schools and the MCC fell into that category.

The public schools had a particular problem. Their staff, such as were fit and of young enough age, had been recruited to fight in the war. The result was that the teaching body was full of older men, in many cases born before the First World War and in some cases during the reign of Queen Victoria. Their values were the values which they had inherited – the destiny of the officer class to lead, the virtues of traditional allegiance to King and country, the ability of those who had received a good education in the classics to take on any job, be it running the Empire or the country, heading a bank or the Army or

Navy, and the belief in the old maxim *mens sana in corpore sano*.

This was the education received (or suffered) by most of the group of amateur batsmen who became the stars of English cricket in the 1950s. It was not just that they, like me, had been brought up to play on wickets which the state schools could hardly ever achieve. We had been brought up to believe that we were there to run the show. In fact, with the honourable exception of David Sheppard, it was many years before we were to be persuaded that the world as conceived by our tutors had changed and that we should change with it. Strangely, the professionals, mostly educated in the state system were also – at least for the most part – conservative in outlook. In my playing days I only found one cricketer in the first-class game with remotely radical views (his nickname, predictably, was 'Red').

If conservatism was fed by education into the young cricketers of the day it was almost part of the biological make-up of MCC members. It is easy to sneer, as some have done, at the inability of the members of the MCC Committees to see that the preservation of amateur status involved a series of flawed measures and was anyway against the grain of the times. But that would be a mistake. These were honest men doing what they honestly believed to be in the best interests of cricket. The fact that hindsight tells us that they were swimming against the tide should not lead us to criticise their good intentions.

Where criticism is reasonable is on two counts. First, it was usually the same people who secured membership of the various committees which were set up. There was very little effort to recruit outsiders to bring in greater knowledge of the non-cricketing world. Secondly, the publicity given to the composition and activities of the committees was shy – to say the least. So little was reported that it is hard to find anybody who was playing first-class cricket at the time, apart from those directly involved in the successive enquiries, who knew that there were any enquiries at all, let alone what they were about. (Ted Dexter only heard about the MCC's final decision that amateurism was to be abolished when he was captaining England in Australia.)

Those criticisms made, there is one element in the prolonged defence of amateurism which needs to be stated clearly. There is no doubt that the motivation of many of those who led the rearguard action was snobbery, an unconscious desire to reaffirm the gentleman/servant or officer/other rank relationship. Sometimes the attempt was made to rationalise this by claiming that amateurs in some way played the game in a different manner from professionals, that they were less risk-averse and more open. When Pelham Warner said of Jack Hobbs that he played 'like an amateur' it was not only meant as a compliment but as an assertion that the amateur's way of playing was in some way superior to that of the professional. It was this which justified the continuing stress on the virtues of amateur captaincy.

It is, of course, possible to indulge in counterfactual speculation. Would May and Cowdrey, for example, have batted differently if they had been professional? Would Trevor Bailey have bowled differently? Would

Denis Compton have batted differently if he had been an amateur? Would Alec Bedser have bowled differently? My instinct would be to say not. But even without such speculation it is possible to find examples by way of demonstration. Both Wally Hammond and Bill Edrich turned amateur; Peter Richardson turned professional; Ted Dexter became a professional when the distinction was abolished; Jim Laker played the final years of his career as an amateur. Yet Hammond's cover drive did not change with his status, nor did Edrich's hook shot or Richardson's on-side delicacy, Dexter's domination of bowlers or Laker's teasing off spin.

The truth, prosaic as it may seem, is that all cricketers of the day – amateur and professional – played as their personality and upbringing demanded. If they were by nature, or nurture, cautious they would be cautious at cricket. If they were, by contrast, flamboyant and outgoing they would be flamboyant and outgoing in their cricket. Compton of Middlesex and John Langridge of Sussex (the one flamboyant and the other – boringly – cautious) were both professionals. Dexter of Sussex and Jimmy Allan of Oxford and Kent (flamboyant and cautious) were both amateurs.

The case in favour of amateur captaincy in the days before Len Hutton became captain of England looks on the face of it to be more substantial. But it is difficult to prove, not least because, with the growth of 'shamateurism', most county captains were professional in all but name. Hutton did indeed bring a degree of rigour into the England captaincy which was followed by May and subsequent England captains. The philosophy prevalent in Yorkshire cricket – that the game is not played for fun – transferred itself to England and down again to the counties in the latter half of the 1950s. Amateur or professional then sang to the same tune.

As for sportsmanship, again held out as an amateur virtue, all evidence is of necessity anecdotal. Nevertheless, in my own experience many of the most sportsmanlike players were professional and some of the least sportsmanlike were amateurs. True, there was less openly demonstrative behaviour on the field than nowadays (raucous appeals, attempts to pressure umpires, exaggerated celebrations at the fall of a wicket and so on) but such developments, however unpleasant they are to traditionalists, might well have occurred anyway.

The fact is that by the late 1950s it was difficult to point to any difference in attitude or behaviour between amateur and professional. With one or two exceptions – Colin Ingleby-Mackenzie was a notable example – the style of captaincy was the same, the intensity of performance was the same, even the dressing-room banter (at least at Essex) was the same. In short, the distinction between gentleman and player, in the old sense, had disappeared.

What had also disappeared, of course, was the financial stability of the county clubs. In spite of all the efforts to create football pools, supporters' clubs, raffles and so on, the fall in attendances was hitting hard. Receipts from television and corporate sponsors were becoming a major part of overall revenue – for the most part collected centrally and distributed onward to county clubs. It is hardly surprising that they opted for a one-day competition to solve their financial problem or that they recognised that it would be incompatible with the preservation of the traditional status of the amateur.

Finally, there was that amorphous 'spirit of the times'. The authority of the officer class, re-established, only partially, during the Second World War, had come under embarrassing scrutiny. By the early 1960s the 'officers', such as they were (many of them ministers in the Macmillan government), had become figures of fun. They could no longer be trusted to run things. The call for 'professionalism' resonated not just in sport but in politics and business. It was Harold Wilson who, as Leader of the Opposition, was able in 1963 to refer to the MCC decision to abolish the amateur/professional distinction as a paradigm for the country as a whole. 'In a country', he declared, 'which has now begun to take cricket seriously enough for even the MCC to abolish the distinction between Gentlemen and Players we are still prepared to allow too much of British industry, on which alone we depend to prevent this country becoming a second class power, to be officered from the pages of *Debrett*.' Even politicians became more professional – the 'knight of the shires' and the 'trade union worthy' gave way to the researcher and the special adviser.

There remains the question of whether the amateur/professional divide enriched or disrupted the first-class game. When he received the news of the abolition of amateur status while in Australia in November 1962, Jim Swanton, the great defender of the faith, 'saw *finis* written to the oldest of all the traditional rivalries of the cricket field.

Not only that, of course. The evolution of the game has been stimulated from its beginnings by the fusion of the two strains, each of which has drawn strength and inspiration from the other. English cricket has been at its best when there has been a reasonably even balance between those who have made the game their livelihood and those who have played it, with whatever degree of application and endeavour, basically for relaxation and enjoyment.'

Swanton's opinion was that of a romantic who saw in the game the epitome of the English summer – the long sunlit days, the clunk of bat on ball, the pint in the pavilion at the end of the day and so on. The problem with that view is that first-class cricket was never like that in the 1950s – if it ever was. Amateur and professional were equally competitive and, when occasion demanded, equally ruthless. Added to that was the influence of the touring sides, particularly the Australians after the Second World War, which gave to Test matches an even greater edge. The mix of modern first-class cricket then became clear with the successes of the Hutton captaincy and has not been – at least in the four- and five-day game – substantially changed since.

It is easy to see, with the clarity of hindsight, that the amateur/professional distinction was, by the end of the 1950s, an anachronism. The spirit of the times, the rise of 'shamateurism', the intrusion of television, the emergence of a new generation of players, all led to what now seems to have been an inevitable conclusion. Yet nobody should doubt the regret which many had (and which some still have) for the passing of the old world. It is an emotion which, when all the argument is over, should command respect, even if the old world never in truth existed.

Acknowledgements

My thanks go to all those who have helped me in what has been a fascinating journey. Pride of place must go to Peter Hennessy, David Cannadine and my former Essex captain, Doug Insole, all of whom have been kind enough to read through drafts and offer informed criticism or fruitful encouragement as occasion demanded. Matt Lyus has been a most diligent and imaginative researcher and Mia Stewart-Wilson has brought her customary expertise to the photographic research. Of my fellow cricketers who have willingly responded to my appeal for witness I thank Bob Barber, Mike Denness, Ted Dexter, Alan Ealham, Charles Fry, Peter Parfitt, Ken Preston, Peter Richardson, Mike (M. J. K.) Smith, Mickey Stewart and Raman Subba Row. No less knowledgeable, and equally helpful, were John Woodcock, Peter Brooke and Neil Robinson (of the MCC Library). Other enthusiasts for the game have contributed their share (I hope they will forgive the omission of titles): David Frost, Eddie Norfolk, Phil Britt, Keith Cook, Adrian Mindin, Bryan Hamblin, Dick Sula and Christopher Arnander. My thanks, too, to the House of Lords Library (and particularly Shorayne Fairweather), the MCC Library (and particularly Charlotte Goodhew and Emma Peplow) and the Arundel archives (Sara Rodgers). Finally, I am as always most grateful to Andrew

Wylie and Tracy Bohan of the Wylie Agency as well as to Alan Samson and Lucinda McNeile at Weidenfeld & Nicolson for enthusiasm and wise advice. I hope that it need hardly be said that I am also deeply indebted to my long-suffering wife Jane who has read through each chapter looking for points, as she says, for the 'ordinary reader' and consequently on many occasions bringing me down to earth from my lovely cloud of cricket jargon.

Index

Moral Re-Armament movement,
15
Moravian Church, 38–9, 72

National Service, 6, 7, 9, 23, 35
abolition, 32
New Zealand, 87
emigrants, 8, 86
New Zealand cricket team, 39,
71, 137, 143
no balls, rules for, 83–4
Noel Gay (Musical Publications)
Ltd, 138, 139, 147
Norfolk, Bernard Fitzalan-
Howard, 16th Duke of:
appearance and character,
111, 112
family, 27, 110
life and works, 109, 110–111
manager of Ashes tour, 111–
13, 117, 169
President of MCC, 113
President of Sussex CCC,
149–50
see also Special (Sub-)
Committee on amateur
status
Northamptonshire County
Cricket Club, 14, 69, 102
captaincy, 69, 72, 73, 102,
138
players' remuneration, 29,
102, 121, 138, 139–40,
147
Subba Row case, 138–40,
148, 158
Nottingham, 13
Nottinghamshire County Cricket
Club, 21, 73, 146

Nugent, Terence, 1st Baron,
168

Old Trafford, 49
Oratory School, The, 110
Osborne, John, *Look Back in
Anger*, 31
Oval, The, 34
dressing rooms, 13, 36, 86
pitches, 55
Oxford, 1–2, 179–80
Oxford University, 5–7, 23, 180
University Parks, 2–3, 179
see also Christ Church
Oxford University Cricket Club
(OUCC), 3, 6, 7–12
Harlequin caps, 3–5
Oxford vs Cambridge
matches, 8, 10, 11–12
selection, 7–8, 9
touring, 10–11

pads and gloves, design of, 84
Pakistan, emigrants, 86
Pakistan cricket team, 50, 53,
56, 71, 142, 164
Palmer, Charles, 28, 114, 124
Parfitt, Peter, 177
Parks, Jim, 46
Payne, A.C., 168
Pearce, Tom, 152, 168
Perks, Reg, 72, 73
Peterborough, 14
Pontypridd, 82
Portal, Charles, 1st Viscount
Portal of Hungerford, 146,
157, 164
Preston, Ken (Casey), 16, 65–6
Prideaux, Roger, 176